Methodism's Racial Dilemma
The Story of the
Central Jurisdiction

Methodism's Racial Dilemma
The Story of the Central Jurisdiction

James S. Thomas

Abingdon Press
Nashville

Methodism's Racial Dilemma:
The Story of the Central Jurisdiction

Copyright © 1992 by Abingdon Press

This book is printed on recycled, acid-free paper.

#24501571

Library of Congress Cataloging-in-Publication Data

Thomas, James S., 1919–
   Methodism's racial dilemma: the story of the Central Jurisdiction
/James S. Thomas.
      p.   cm.
   Includes bibliographical references and index.
   ISBN 0-687-37129-5 (alk. paper)
   1. Methodist Church (U.S.) Central Jurisdiction—History.
2. Methodist Church—United States—History—20th century. 3. Afro
-American Methodists—History—20th century. 4. Race relations-
-Religious aspects—Methodists. 5. Race relations—United States.
I. Title.
BX8435.T52
287'.631'08996073—dc20   91-35951
                                                                                    CIP

MANUFACTURED IN THE UNITED STATES OF AMERICA

This is for Ruth.

C O N T E N T S

I n 1953, Dwight W. Culver published his research entitled "Negro Segregation in the Methodist Church." At that time he made two statements that are important as background for this book.

First, Culver said that "The Methodist Church has more Negro members than the other 'white' denominations in the United States combined."[1] This fact alone, the fact of relative numbers of one race to another, makes it important to study the Central Jurisdiction of The Methodist Church. In what ways were African Americans and whites related in terms of structure? What was the background of social attitudes and practices that made a racially segregated structure inevitable at the time of Methodist Union? By what means was the racial jurisdiction finally included in the geographic jurisdictions of The Methodist Church? All of these are important questions which this book seeks to answer.

Second, Culver said:

> The largest Protestant denomination in the United States is seen to have developed its own peculiar adaptations to segregationist demands. Its patterns of segregation are as complex and its rationalizations as interesting as those of the secular society in which it operated.[2]

In this book attention is given to "the secular society in which [the Methodist Church] operate[s]." While racial segregation had been challenged in the courts—including the Supreme Court—the massive legal structure which sup-

9

ported segregation had hardly been dented in 1939. The aspirations of African Americans for full and extensive citizenship were hardly known to the powers that existed in church and state. Indeed, as late as 1944, it was considered necessary to write a book on *What the Negro Wants*.

This book on the Central Jurisdiction is written with three types of readers in mind.

First, there are many ministers and laypersons who spent a significant part of their lives as members of the Central Jurisdiction. It is my hope that this study will be an aid to their reflection upon events and resolutions that came to their attention, both in the Central Jurisdiction and in the General Conference.

Second, many younger ministers and lay persons never lived and served in the Central Jurisdiction. The story of this racial structure has been shared with them often in the recollection of events, less often in written form. It is the purpose of this book to provide a perspective in which they can understand both the history of events and the African American Methodists of The United Methodist Church.

Third, this book is written for those who have heard of the Central Jurisdiction, but have never become acquainted with its nature or its development. If researchers are among these persons, it is my hope that some of the sources given in this book will lead them to further study of the Central Jurisdiction. But this book is not written primarily for scholars. Rather, it is written to tell a story, a story of a dilemma that was finally resolved as far as church structure is concerned.

The personal story of the writer was the major reason for the writing of this book. In 1939, when the Methodist Plan of Union was adopted, I graduated from college. I heard many conversations about the Plan of Union, but none of them really came alive for me. In 1940, when I met the first African American bishop who came to preside over my native South

Carolina Conference, I was deeply impressed. When I entered seminary later that year, there were more discussions about the Central Jurisdiction and the new "arrangements that were made for us."

When I became a pastor in 1944, I was aware of little more than the name "Central Jurisdiction" and the fact that we had our own bishop who lived nearer to us than the white bishops who had come from great distances before 1939.

It was only when I became a staff member of the General Board of Education and traveled widely throughout the Jurisdiction that I began to enter into lively discussions about the segregation of the Central Jurisdiction. Like others in the Central Jurisdiction, I wrote articles, spoke against segregation in both church and state, and offered some alternatives to the racial structure.

This may have led to my appointment to and chairmanship of the Committee of Five in 1960. I have tried to tell the story of that committee's work in the pages that follow.

In sum, then, I grew up in the church with a keen awareness of the Central Jurisdiction as a segregated structure. I spent twenty-four years in the Central Jurisdiction—1940–1964. After going to Iowa as one of the two bishops to be a resident in and president of a predominantly white annual conference, I served twelve years in the Iowa Area and twelve years in the Ohio East Area. So I also spent twenty-four years in the North Central Jurisdiction.

In the course of writing this book, I became indebted to many people. I want to express my appreciation to Dr. W. Astor Kirk, Secretary of the Committee of Five, for his helpful suggestions of resources and his encouragement along the way; to Mrs. Ann Ralston, who typed the entire manuscript; to Dean James E. Kirby, Jr., of Perkins School of Theology, for his helpful corrections and suggestions; to Dr. Grant S. Shockley, for his help in providing valuable resource material; to Dr. Robert Maloy and Mr. Roger Loyd of

Bridwell Library at Perkins School of Theology for the provision of most helpful library space and resources; to Bishops O. Eugene Slater, W. T. Handy, and John Wesley Hardt for their constant encouragement and support; to Dr. Harlan London of Syracuse University for reading parts of the manuscript and offering helpful suggestions; to Mrs. Dovie Patrick of the Clark Atlanta University Library for permitting the use of the James P. Brawley papers on the Central Jurisdiction; to Dr. Zan W. Holmes, Jr. and Mrs. Timothy Echols for sharing with me some important unpublished papers on the Central Jurisdiction; and to my wife, Ruth, for the many hours during which she encouraged me and kept me at it.

The writer is aware of the many limitations of this book. Those who assisted me are in no way responsible for its limitations. The story is so easily told as oral history that the writing of it seems difficult indeed. As hard as I tried to incorporate all the helpful suggestions I received, I am sure I missed some opportunities for improvement. There comes a time when the story must be told as best as the writer can tell it, and that is what I have tried to do. If this account tells a story well enough to encourage others to write other stories in their own way, I shall be grateful.

NOTES

1. Dwight W. Culver, *Negro Segregation in The Methodist Church* (New Haven: Yale University Press, 1953), p. vii.
2. Ibid., p. ix.

1

Beginning a
New Journey

When John and Charles Wesley founded the Holy Club at Oxford University in 1729, they did not know that they were also planting the seeds for a large denomination, the Methodist Church, in America. But that is how the bishops of the Methodist Episcopal Church, many years afterward, introduced the members of the church to Methodism.

In the early years of American Methodism, the bishops gave a brief historical statement at the beginning of the *Discipline*. They wanted all members to know at least a little of the story of John and Charles Wesley:

> In 1729, two young men, in England, reading the Bible, saw they could not be saved without holiness: followed after it, and incited others to do so. In 1737, they saw, likewise, that men are justified before they are sanctified: but still holiness was their object. God then thrust them out to raise a holy people.[1]

If the holy people raised by the Wesleys had remained a small sect, shut away from the world, the Methodist Church in America might not have faced some of its dilemmas that came later. But John Wesley made it clear that holiness, for him, meant *social* holiness. The hungry were to be fed, greed was to be checked, industry was to be just, and slavery was to end. Throughout his ministry in England, Wesley preached and lived a gospel of social holiness. At the same time, he lived out a deep personal piety.

The Long Shadow of Slavery

In mid-eighteenth-century England and America, slavery was one of the most evil social systems Wesley faced. When John and Charles founded the Holy Club in 1729, the institution of slavery in the colonies was already more than one hundred years old. It would have been easy enough for Wesley to have considered slavery to be ordained of God, and thus eternal.

Instead, John Wesley became more and more convinced that slavery was a social evil that could not be tolerated. He was so moved by his convictions that in 1773, at the age of seventy, he sent a preliminary draft of his tract *Thoughts upon Slavery* to a friend, and a year later the tract was published.

It was not long before copies of Wesley's tract were widely distributed, both in England and in America. Wesley left no doubt as to what he was saying:

O burst thou all their chains in sunder: Thou Saviour of all, make them free, that they may be free indeed.[2]

This statement could have been interpreted to mean "make the slave spiritually free even as he or she remained a good slave." But anyone who read the entire tract would not miss its meaning. Wesley's witness on the slavery issue would be made even more clear in his later life and writings.

Within a week of his death in 1791, John Wesley made a final statement on human slavery. He wrote a letter to William Wilberforce, who was fighting a stiff battle to abolish the slave trade in England. His encouraging words to Wilberforce took nothing away from his earlier view that slavery was an evil that the human race could no longer bear. This is what he wrote:

before the separate racial jurisdiction actually became a fact. It was the issue of slavery that fueled the great abolitionist debates of the early nineteenth century. This same issue was at the center of the General Conference of 1844, which ended with a division of the Methodist Church, North and South. Slavery cast a long shadow.

Any American Methodists who read Wesley's writings faced the dilemma of proving slavery to be right when Wesley had declared it so palpably wrong. And it was not so much that Wesley's word should be law. In addition, there was the witness of the Bible, especially the teachings of Jesus; there was the bad experience of slavery in England; and there were the many cases of inhumanity, slaveholder to slave, that made the defense of slavery increasingly difficult. True, the institution of slavery lasted for a very long time, but Methodist defenders of slavery could take no comfort in the example of their founder. John Wesley's witness and writings became a part of the self-definition of Methodism.

Slavery in America

On October 27, 1771, Francis Asbury landed at Philadelphia. His work in the States was highly productive. In 1784, John Wesley wrote a letter to his "American Methodists" telling them that he had appointed Asbury and Thomas Coke as joint superintendents "over our brethren in North America." They therefore became the first bishops of the Methodist Church.

Asbury found some beginnings of Methodism in North America but he became the one whose mission and vigor would give new life to the early Methodist movement. His goal was to "reform the continent and spread scriptural holiness over the land." In fulfilling this charge, he became the chief architect of American Methodism.

Methodists in the colonies inherited their vigorous

opposition to slavery from Mr. Wesley. Both Thomas Coke and Francis Asbury were strong opponents of slavery. George Whitefield, a famous evangelist who was associated with Mr. Wesley, saw things differently. He never opposed slavery and actually held slaves himself.

In the spring of 1780, Francis Asbury held a conference in Baltimore. A statement on slavery came before the conference. The preachers claimed that slavery was contrary to divine and human justice. It was, they proclaimed, against the Golden Rule. In 1783, the Virginia Conference followed the example of the Baltimore Conference. The sentiment grew. By the spring of 1784, circuit riders voted to expel members who held slaves.

Whatever victory the preachers saw in this rule to expel slaveholders could not be celebrated for long. By June of 1785, another Conference at Baltimore suspended the rule on behalf of the entire church. What one group of preachers had so strongly supported in one session could not withstand the fire storm of opposition that came from the other side.[4] Thus began what Donald O. Mathews called "Compromise and Conscience."

It was a pattern that would follow the church throughout most of its history. John Wesley had declared American slavery "vile." That is hardly a term on which compromise can easily be reached. Now, before the realities of the North American situation, a compromise was not only reached but later justified and supported by both custom and the Bible. In any case, the issue of slavery would not go away.

Abolition: Voices For and Against

In spite of all attempts to still the voices of opposition to slavery, they continued to be heard. Muted for a time in one place, these voices cried out in another.

The first Methodist Anti-Slavery Society was formed in

1832 in Lynn, Massachusetts. Ten years earlier, the British Anti-Slavery Society was formed. Its influence supported the aggressive leadership of William Lloyd Garrison, and others associated with him.

This was almost fifty years after the first Methodist Compromise on the issue of slavery and may indicate the power of the pro-slavery sentiment during the latter part of the eighteenth century and the first thirty years of the nineteenth.

The message of the abolitionist was simple. Richard Cameron writes: "One of the first concerns of the abolitionist was to counter the apologetic for slavery. . . . The sum and substance of what they had to say was: slavery is unjust, it is sinful, and it should be stopped."[5] This message, simple though it was, ran headon into a completely opposite point of view.

During the 1830s and 1840s the abolitionists were very active, producing some of the most dramatic events in the life of the church. Some of the most prominent of the Methodist abolitionists were Orange Scott, Lucius Matlock, Abel Stevens, and Wilbur Fisk. These men, and other leaders with them, used every argument that they could find to convince the Methodist Church that slavery was sin and had to be stopped. Abel Stevens used the influential pages of *Zion's Herald,* of which he was editor, to that end.

Orange Scott, a native of Vermont, is an outstanding example of the power of the abolitionist movement within The Methodist Church. Born in 1800, he joined the New England Conference in 1822. With a formal schooling of only thirteen months, he largely educated himself and learned to speak and write with great skill. His passion for the anti-slavery cause was shown in many ways, including an able address to the General Conference of 1836. In 1837 he declined to take an appointment, working instead as an agent of the American Anti-Slavery Society. Finally, by 1842, he gave up hope that the Methodist Church would ever end its deep investment in slavery. He then left the church and led himself and others into a new church: The Wesleyan Methodist Connection. As it later turned out, this was to be only one of several schisms or defections from the Methodist Church because of slavery. The long shadow of slavery, after two centuries of existence, fell over the church and the nation as well. Given the divided points of view in the church, the Methodist abolitionists found many opponents. Slavery was a highly controversial issue and many leaders recognized its divisive potential long before the General Conference of 1844. On May 1, 1844, one writer described the situation as a battle between extreme points of view:

> We have not attempted to conceal the fact that some portions of our Connection have been greatly agitated on the question of slavery, and that the conflict of parties has, in this instance, as in most others, driven the antagonists to opposite extremes; that we must expect to find in the General Conference two contrary ultraisms represented.[6]

One letter to the editor of *The Christian Advocate and Journal* recognized what he considered to be the extreme position of *Zion's Herald*. He wrote, with thinly veiled disgust: "*Zion's Herald* is crowded to suffocation with response to the call for another Anti-Slavery Convention in the New England Conference."[7]

A special attitude toward human beings was adopted by the anti-slavery societies. There were those who felt (and said) that one human being should not hold another in slavery. For them, this belief was soundly based on the Bible and the clear example of Jesus Christ in his attitude toward human beings.

So strongly did the abolitionists press their case that preserving the unity of the church became a continuing problem. Looking back on the General Conference of 1836, the succeeding General Conference opened on a note that discouraged further enactments on slavery.

> We cannot withhold from you, at this eventful period, the solemn conviction of our minds, that no new ecclesiastical legislation on the subject of slavery, at this time, will have a tendency to accomplish these more desirable aspects.[8]

But it was not to be so. In that same General Conference, the fraternal delegate from the British Wesleyan Conference addressed the issue in such a way that it could hardly be avoided. Referring to an address delivered four years earlier, and affirming that they still held the same views expressed then, he said that they were more confirmed in their views of the moral evil of slavery. Then he went on to say:

> Far be it from us to advocate violent or ill-considered measures. We are, however, strongly and unequivocally of opinion that it is . . . the paramount Christian duty of ministers . . . in your country to maintain the principle of the opposition to slavery with earnest zeal, and unflinching firmness.[9]

The British Wesleyans held that slavery was a great moral evil. This was a page from Wesley's *Thoughts upon Slavery,* and it did not help those who wanted to keep slavery from dividing the church.

A second view toward slavery was that the institution was compatible with Christian doctrine and should cause no disturbance to the conscience.

Looking back upon the 1930s, John A. Faulkner, a professor at Drew Theological Seminary, stated:

> Many thousand Methodist laymen and ministers owned slaves with as little qualm of conscience as they owned horses.

To attack the institution as both unchristian and unpatriotic might lead to a disruption of the church as well as of the state.[10]

This was a long way from Wesley's position, but there is no doubt it expressed the way some people looked upon slaves. Clearly, these opposite attitudes toward human slavery were very deep and persuasive. To challenge one or the other was only to deepen the view held by the one who felt the need to defend his position. The bishops saw this divisive possibility and tried to keep the General Conference of 1836 and 1840 as far away from debates on slavery as they could.

There were, generally speaking, three dominant attitudes expressed on human slavery during the 1830s and 1840s.

The first was the view expressed by John Wesley, so powerfully in his tract, and reiterated in his letter to Wilberforce in 1791. It was a view that was rejected many times—but it kept coming back. Prophetic voices would not leave it silent.

Not long after Wesley's death in March of 1791, the British House of Commons debated the possibility of abolition. Wilberforce's motion failed at that time. There was a partial victory in 1807, but it was not until August 1, 1838, over forty years after Wesley's death, that British slaves were finally emancipated.

A second and opposite view was that expressed by many slaveholders. There were those who held that slavery was right. They had no more qualm of conscience about holding a slave than they had about owning a horse. They were born into the institution, found it profitable, both economically and socially, and saw no reason to change it.

Even where there might have been qualms of conscience there were rationalizations of many kinds, including those of Christians. The Georgia Conference held that if slavery was not a positive good, it was certainly not a positive evil. This statement removed the necessity of proving anything. The institution was simply declared morally neutral and therefore as much beyond the jurisdiction of a church as it was within the blessings of the state.

A third view toward human slavery was that held by those who felt helpless to abolish the institution and also to care for the soul of the slave owner, too. They would do their best to improve the condition of the slave as a slave person, but they would not abolish slavery.

On May 2, 1844, at the opening of the General Conference, Bishop Joshua Soule spoke for the bishops of the church. He said:

> We may preach the gospel of Christ to them, unite them in the communion of his Church, and introduce them to a participation of the blessings of her fellowship, and thus be instruments of their preparation for the riches of the inheritance of the saints in glory. This, as ministers of Christ, is our work, and should be our glory and joy. This, by the grace of God helping us, we can do; but to raise them to equal rights and privileges is not within our power. Let us not labor in vain nor spend our strength for naught.[11]

After 225 years of existence in America, the institution of slavery must have seemed to be invincible to many people. They would preach the gospel to the slaves and do whatever else seemed to be within reason for them, but it would be spending "strength for naught" to attempt anything more.

This attitude was expressed by one who wrote a letter to the editor of *The Christian Advocate and Journal* in August of 1844. T. J. Deyerle gave the editor his view in this statement:

> Could I rescue the slave to freedom, to independence, to the rights, to all the rights of man, I would most gladly do it. But this I cannot do—you cannot do. And if I cannot burst the bonds of the colored man, I will not strengthen them. If I

cannot extend to him all the good I would, I will not shut him out from the benefits which I have in my power to bestow.[12]

No doubt there were many well-meaning people who agreed. They could see no way to abolish slavery, but they would do what they could to make the bondage more bearable.

Mission to the Slaves in America

As early as 1701, there was expressed interest in the evangelization of the slaves. The Society for the Propagation of the Gospel in Foreign Parts was established in London in that year. One of its purposes was to do missionary work among "the heathen," especially Negroes and Indians. The Society felt this to be important and contacted a number of influential churchmen to impress them with the need for missionary work. For all of its good intentions, this work did not meet with much success.

The slaveholders were not interested in missionary work among their slaves for two main reasons, among others. First, many slaveholders did not believe that the slaves were souls that needed to be saved. Putting it bluntly, they felt that the slave was more animal than human. Second, the fear of slave insurrection was ever in the mind of the slaveholder. Any chances that the slave would think of himself as anything more than a slave could be dangerous.

During John Wesley's time in Georgia, he did not have contact with large groups of African Americans. But in one month, while at sea, Wesley recorded in his journal two times when he instructed at least one African American who was on board:

"I began instructing a negro lad in the principles of Christianity." (Mon. December 20, 1737)

"I began to read and explain some passages of the Bible to the young negro." (Sat. January 7, 1738)[13]

The use of the term "the young negro" suggests that Wesley might have instructed the same person twice. This could hardly be called a mission to slaves, but it was an example of what could be done with illiterate people who, for everyone's good, could gain some insight into the Bible.

The Methodists, however, became highly successful in their missions to the slaves. Forty percent of the Methodists in South Carolina and Georgia were slaves in 1826. The Reverend James O. Andrew of Georgia, later to be a bishop in the forefront of the controversy, accused the church of negligence in the face of so great an opportunity. He urged the church to greater action and found support along the way.

In 1829, Charles Cotesworth Pinckney, seeing the good of Methodist influence upon the slaves of a neighboring plantation, asked the South Carolina Conference to send several preachers to his plantation. Pinckney later became lieutenant governor and then governor of South Carolina and was highly respected among citizens of the state. Other plantation owners quickly followed his example.

The man who did the most to establish a successful mission to slaves was the Reverend William Capers of South Carolina. Capers himself was an educated man. He attended the University of South Carolina; and then, against the advice of his presiding elder, went on to study divinity. He was president of the South Carolina Conference Missionary Society at the time that Pinckney requested missionaries to the slaves. He became editor of the *Southern Christian Advocate* and used that position, as he had others, to influence his conference toward missions. He was a slaveholder himself but is described, by one writer, as a benevolent man: "To him a slave was a soul to be valued, a human being ultimately equal to his master, even if 'uncontrollable circumstances' effaced that equality in society."[14]

The mission to the slaves became a holy passion with William Capers. Earlier, in his ministry at Charleston, South Carolina, he had sent African American preachers to the slaves even though that, at the time, was an illegal act. Appraising the mission to the slaves from this time in history is not the point of this review. Within the context of its time, the mission to the slaves demonstrated one clear fact of vital importance. The slave was a human being, not a beast of burden to be held with no qualm of conscience. Capers believed that the slave could learn and wrote a simple catechism to aid that learning.

By his ministry, and that of others, Capers joined eighty Methodist missionaries caring for 22,000 slaves. That was the direct statistical result of their work. What could not be measured were the wider effects of these missions, the indirect contacts of slave with slave and missionary with slave.

Measured against the standard of slavery, as it was then practiced, the mission to the slaves was as high a point as most slaveholders ever reached. But measured against John Wesley's standard, as he wrote in his letter to Wilberforce, the mission to slaves fell far short of full fellowship in Jesus Christ. The purpose of the mission was laudable—to improve, even to make a good slave. Wesley's goal, however, was to emancipate, to free these human beings for a fuller life. It is a significant fact that, at least for a brief time and in a few places, African American and white worshipers shared the life of the church without distinction. H. Richard Niebuhr wrote that "white and black worshipped together and, at their best, sought to realize the brotherhood Jesus had practiced and Paul had preached."[15] Nor was this free association of the races limited to local churches. Carter G. Woodson reports that in the 1840s, several Baptist Associations had both African American and white members. In fact, the African

Americans were not permitted to separate from whites. Then he went on to say that "No distinction was made between the members of the two races in the minutes of the Association [to which these churches belonged]."[16]

This was not the first time that African Americans and whites had worshiped in the same church, but the earlier pattern was strict segregation. Indeed, fully integrated worship was so rare and so little a part of history that many people, then as now, doubt if it ever existed at all. Yet in one of those strange paradoxes of American race relations, there was, at least for a brief time, integrated worship, instances of black pastors to white worshipers, and many more cases of black preachers preaching to white congregations. One such example was Samuel R. Ward, a Presbyterian who pastored a white church in South Butler, New York.[17]

Separation, Black from White

If what was practiced for a brief time in at least a few places, when African Americans and whites worshiped together without distinctions or discrimination, had become the dominant pattern of worship, instead of a strange departure from the norm, the Methodist Episcopal Church would have become a very different kind of church. There would have been no need for separate African American Annual Conferences and, later, a racially defined Central Jurisdiction.

The early zeal of Methodists to evangelize the slaves brought many of them into the Societies and into the classes. They were enrolled without regard to race or to their slave status. Their names were on the membership rolls of churches in New York, New Jersey, Delaware, and Pennsylvania, to name a few. They were members of these local churches, in full fellowship.

What happened to this brief period of unsegregated

worship also happened to the high resolve on slavery in 1780: it became a casualty of the prevailing customs and laws in the United States. Conscience prompted this island of full fellowship in a sea of slavery and segregation, but compromise took over and segregation within a slave society became the norm, the order of the day, causing the separation of black from white.

The prevailing pattern which evolved was that of mixed worship with segregation. In earlier days, this mixed worship might well have been as much a matter of keeping an eye on the slaves as it was concern for their souls. However, in later days, slaves and free African Americans worshiped in the same churches with whites. There were, however, at least a few radical departures from the norm. One pioneer African American preacher, Lemuel Haynes, successfully pastored a white Congregational Church in Connecticut as early as the 1780s. No such example can be found in the early history of the Methodist Episcopal Church.[18]

In spite of these limitations on worship, there were African American members of St. George's Church, Methodist Episcopal, in Philadelphia. They resented the segregation that kept them from full fellowship, but accepted it for a time. If they had chosen to become Baptist, they could have joined one of the many African American Baptist Churches that had been organized by that time. But they wanted to remain Methodists. The same things that appealed to them as they became Methodists continued to hold them within the church: a powerful but simple message of a loving God whose concern extended to all people; a memory of the zeal of the preachers who evangelized them; an expression of conscience on slavery, albeit a muted one by 1787. These reasons may also explain why some African Americans remained with the Methodist Episcopal Church throughout all of its changes.

The precipitating event for separation occurred on a Sunday in 1787. Richard Allen, a free African American member of St. George's Church, was joined by two other members of the church as they chose seats in the main section of the sanctuary. A zealous sexton, overlooking the fact that these African American members usually sat on seats placed around the main floor, rudely attempted to force them to sit in the gallery. The fact that this incident occurred during prayer only underscores its shame.

This is the way Allen describes the incident:

> A number of us usually sat on seats placed around the wall, and on Sabbath morning we went to church, and the sexton stood at the door and told us to go in the gallery. He told us to go and we would see where to sit. We expected to take the seats over the ones we formerly occupied below, not knowing any better. We took those seats. Meeting had begun, and they were nearly done singing, and just as we got to the seats the elder said, "Let us pray." We had not been long upon our knees before I heard considerable scuffling and loud talking. I raised my head up and saw one of the trustees, H—— M——, having hold of the Rev. Absalom Jones, pulling him off his knees, and saying, "You must get up; you must not kneel here." Mr. Jones replied, "Wait until prayer is over." Mr. H—— M—— said, "No, you must get up now, or I will call for aid and force you away." Mr. Jones said, "Wait until prayer is over, and I will get up and trouble you no more." With that he beckoned to one of the other trustees, Mr. L—— S——, to come to his assistance. He came and went to William White to pull him up. By this time prayer was over, and we all went out of the church in a body, and they were no more plagued by us in the church. This raised a great excitement and inquiry among the citizens, insomuch that I believe they were ashamed of their conduct.[19]

This profoundly moving incident was a watershed in the religious life of African Americans. Richard Allen and others rented a storeroom where they could worship by themselves. This did not please the elders of St. George's Church. The same people who forced Allen and his friends from their knees during prayer actually had the pious temerity to threaten them with expulsion from the membership of St. George's Church if they did not desist from their efforts to find a separate place for worship. In spite of these threats, Allen and his friends continued their efforts to find a separate place in which to worship with dignity.

These efforts to form a separate African American Methodist Church have other points of drama. If such a church was to be formed, to what denomination could it attach itself? Allen and his friend Absalom Jones were licensed local preachers in the Methodist Episcopal Church. They were still pursued by the elders of St. George's Church, but they saw no way to return since they "were treated so scandalously." It was apparent that Allen and Jones were strong personalities, each with a following among the people.

The majority of their followers favored going to the Episcopal Church. Absalom Jones went with the majority. He was ordained deacon of the Episcopal Church. In 1804 he was ordained a priest, the first African American to be ordained a priest in the Protestant Episcopal Church.[20]

It is remarkable, almost a minor miracle, that Allen remained a Methodist. He had suffered the same indignity along with Absalom Jones. His loyalty to the church would not seem to overbalance the hurt of forced segregation. Yet his love for the theology of the Methodist Church, and his memory of the attitude of some kindly whites were enough to hold him steady. As it turned out, remaining Methodist in polity and theology meant much more than remaining Methodist in the rudely expressed spirit of St. George's Church.

It was the spirit and integrity of Richard Allen that attracted followers. Born on February 16, 1760, he, along with his family, was the slave of Benjamin Chew, of Philadelphia.

Eventually, Allen joined a Methodist society that met in

the forest. He was a very loyal Methodist in every way. Deeply religious, Allen persuaded his new master to have preaching in the home. One of the preachers was Freeborn Garrettson, a strong opponent of slavery. Garrettson preached so powerfully that the master was profoundly impressed. Not long after that house service, the master allowed Richard Allen and his brother to purchase their freedom for two thousand dollars in Continental money.

As a child, Allen was sold, along with his family, to a new master in Dover, Delaware. Eventually this new master fell heavily in debt and he sold Allen's mother and three of the children to a man named Stokeley. Parts of the Allen family may have been sold as early as 1768.

According to Allen, his new master was a good man, "being more like a father to his slaves than anything else." In this home atmosphere, there were no longer slaves, but field workers.

Allen's master permitted two of his brothers to leave the farm and go where they could find work. Eventually Allen earned enough money to buy his freedom. With this new freedom, he made his way to New Jersey, where he spent several months, and then to Philadelphia.

This was the Richard Allen who was so profoundly impressed by the incident of segregation in St. George's Methodist Episcopal Church—a church dedicated by Bishop Asbury in 1794. Still, there was a great need to unify the separate groups of African Americans in various churches.

In an attempt to create this unity, Richard Allen and another strong leader, Daniel Coker, called a meeting in Philadelphia in April of 1816. Out of this meeting came the African Methodist Episcopal Church. It was the beginning of the major independent church movement among African Americans in the United States.

Richard Allen became the unquestioned leader of this group and was elected a bishop on April 11, 1816. The denomination grew under Allen's leadership. Within two years there were sixteen charges, stretching from Charleston, South Carolina to Philadelphia. The total membership was 6,757.

Between the shameful incident in St. George's Church in 1787 and the beginning of a separate church for African Americans, almost thirty years passed. Within the decade after the founding of the African Methodist Episcopal Church, a former member of Zion Church in New York City was sent to establish a church there. Not being fully in accord with Bishop Allen's desire to expand, a Society of Zion Church members was formed and the African Methodist Episcopal Zion Church was the result. In 1822, this church had grown to a membership of 9,888 with 140 preachers.

By now, the separation of black from white, though not yet complete, was well underway. Whatever white Methodists thought, African Americans were making it clear that, for many of them, segregation was extremely distasteful.

While segregation was no less distasteful for many other African American Methodists, they remained within the structure of the Methodist Episcopal Church. No writer has ever been able to explain adequately why so many African Americans made this choice. But perhaps it can be understood that in spite of its compromise on the slavery issue as a denomination, and in spite of the St. George's Church incident, the Methodist Episcopal Church has always had individual prophets who kept hope alive among the African American membership. Moreover, from the beginning, there were African Americans in the Methodist Episcopal Church and it is easy to see why a substantial number of these members continued to feel they belonged to it.

From 1780 to 1816, the state of American race relations could almost be explained in two words: slavery and segregation. It was these two issues that began a major difference of opinion among Methodists and it was these two issues which eventually caused the Great Separation in 1844 and the Central Jurisdiction in 1939.

NOTES

1. *The Doctrines and Discipline of the Methodist Episcopal Church* (New York: C. Lane and C. B. Tippett, 1844), p. 3.
2. Warren Thomas Smith, *John Wesley and Slavery* (Nashville: Abingdon Press, 1986), p. 148.
3. Albert Outler, ed., *John Wesley* (New York: Oxford University Press, 1964), pp. 85-86.
4. See Donald G. Mathews, *Slavery and Methodism* (Princeton: Princeton University Press, 1965), pp. 11-13.
5. Richard M. Cameron, "The Abolitionist Struggle in the Methodist Episcopal Church," Emory Stevens Bucke, ed., *The History of American Methodism*, Vol. II (Nashville: Abingdon Press, 1964), p. 29.
6. *The Christian Advocate and Journal*, May 1, 1844.
7. Ibid., January 17, 1844.
8. *Journal of the General Conference of the Methodist Episcopal Church*, 1840, p. 136.
9. Ibid., pp. 152-53.
10. Essay by John A. Faulkner, "The History of Various Separations," in *A Working Conference on the Union of American Methodism* (New York: The Methodist Book Concern, 1916), p. 22.
11. *Journal of the General Conference of the Methodist Episcopal Church*, 1844, p. 165.
12. *The Christian Advocate and Journal*, August 28, 1844.
13. *The Journal of John Wesley*, as abridged by Nehemiah Cornock (New York: Capricorn Books, 1963), pp. 33-34.
14. Mathews, *Slavery and Methodism*, p. 68.
15. H. Richard Niebuhr, *The Social Sources of Denominationalism* (New York: Living Age Books, 1957), p. 247.
16. Carter G. Woodson, *The History of the Negro Church* (Washington, D.C.: The Associated Publishers, 1945), p. 98.
17. Ibid., p. 160.
18. Ibid., p. 54.
19. See Harry V. Richardson, *Dark Salvation* (Garden City, N.Y.: Anchor Press, 1976), p. 72.
20. Ibid., p. 73.

C H A P T E R 2

The Increasing Dilemma

U nless one remembers that the making of the American mind began long before the founding of the nation, one will not understand the patterns and structures of racial segregation. In 1619, a Dutch ship brought twenty "Negers" to the colonies and sold them to the planters to work in the tobacco fields. This established slavery in the colonies 170 years before the ratification of the Constitution in 1789. So powerful did the institution of slavery become, that it seemed to some an eternal institution.

To others, slavery was as unnatural as it was prevalent, as destructive of humanity as it was productive of wealth, and could not be justified in a Christian and democratic nation. Among them were the seeds of the abolitionist movement— and emancipation.

Now comes the dilemma, a situation in which any alternative for solution is fraught with problems. Methodist bishops had done their best to hold the abolitionists at least at arm's length. In their episcopal address to the General Conference of 1840, they said "that the interests of religion would not be advanced by any additional enactments in regard to it [slavery]."[1]

This statement was a clear misreading of the sentiment of the General Conference of 1840. Instead of "no further legislation," there was a deluge of no fewer than fifty-five petitions and memorials on the question of slavery. All of these were referred to the Committee on Slavery of the General Conference.

The Committee on Slavery, under the Chairmanship of Nathan Bangs, did not relish the task of preparing a report on slavery. On Thursday, May 14, 1840, slavery report number one was presented to the General Conference. The report read as follows:

> N. Bangs, Chairman of the Committee on Slavery reported in part, that that committee, at present, cannot act on any of the subjects referred to them in the Bishops' Address touching the acts of the Annual Conferences on the subject of slavery and abolitionism, and asking to be discharged from the further consideration of all such matters as properly come before the Committee on Itinerancy.[2]

No sooner had that report been made than a motion prevailed by H. A. Leigh "to recommit to the Committee on Slavery." The motion prevailed. It became clear that the General Conference of 1840 would hear more than some of the members wanted to hear on the issue of slavery.

Many people sought other ways out of the dilemma created by 221 years of slavery. To some, the solution was colonization. On Monday, May 18, a resolution came before the General Conference:

> Resolved, by the delegates of the several Annual Conferences in the General Conference assembled, that we view with favor the efforts which are now making by the American Colonization Society to build up a colony on the coast of Africa with the free people of colour, by their own consent.[3]

However well-meaning this resolution was, it became all but lost in the many petitions on slavery, pro and con. There was no way to keep the topic of slavery out of primary consideration by the General Conference of 1840.

This was a disappointment to many. After all, the issue of slavery had been successfully compromised or avoided for the almost sixty years since the high ground on slavery taken in the Christmas Conference of 1784. The divisive potential of the issue was already clear, and perhaps many well-meaning members, North and South, only hoped to avoid or delay the outright confrontation that was finally inevitable.

Whatever was reported by the Committee on Slavery would occasion hot and maybe, also, acrimonious debate. The time for taking sides was rapidly approaching and there was no way to escape a dilemma.

The Great Separation

The ninth delegated General Conference of the Methodist Episcopal Church met in New York City on Wednesday, May 1, 1844. When the Conference was organized there was no provision for a Committee on Slavery. On Friday, May 3, J. A. Collins, of the Baltimore Annual Conference, moved for the appointment "of a committee to be called the Committee on Slavery, and to be constituted by one member from each Annual Conference." William Capers, of the South Carolina Conference, moved to lay the motion on the table, but the motion was lost and a Committee on Slavery was ordered.[4]

With the authorization of a Committee on Slavery, thirteen petitions or memorials were presented in rapid-fire order. Since several of the same petitions came from a number of local churches, the thirteen could easily have become thirty-nine or forty. Other petitions came from entire annual conferences—New York, New Hampshire, and Philadelphia being among them. After the presentation of the first thirteen petitions, many others followed.

On Saturday, May 4, the Committee on Slavery was appointed. Among the members of the Committee was Peter Cartwright of Illinois, whose name had already become famous in the Methodist Episcopal Church. On Monday, May 6, the General Conference heard a resolution on the alteration of the rule on slavery. That rule, written in italics for emphasis, appeared among the General Rules which John Wesley designed for the Methodist Societies, first in Europe and then in America. In the prefix to the rule, Mr. Wesley said:

> It is therefore expected of all who continue therein [the Methodist societies], that they continue to evidence their desire of salvation . . . by avoiding evil of every kind, especially that which is most generally practiced, such as . . . "the buying and selling of men, women and children, with the intention to enslave them."[5]

When the time for petitions, memorials, and resolutions had ended, W. A. Smith, of the Virginia Annual Conference, presented a resolution of instruction to the Committee on Slavery. On motion of J. Spencer this resolution of instruction was laid on the table by a vote of eighty-eight to seventy-eight. It became clear, that (1) this was a divided General Conference, and (2) slavery would be an issue that could no longer be avoided. Slavery was a denominational issue at the beginning of the General Conference of 1844 and continued to be to its end.

With differences of opinion already indicated by votes in smaller groups, and with slavery now squarely before it, the General Conference of 1844 needed only an occasion to bring about confrontation. That occasion came on Tuesday, May 7.

F. A. Harding, a minister of the Baltimore Conference, had been suspended from ministerial standing in the conference because he refused to manumit slaves that came into his possession by marriage. He appealed to the General Conference. On motion of Samuel Luckey of the Genesee Conference and J. B. Finley of the Ohio Conference, the appeal was admitted and entertained. There was now no escape from confrontation.[6]

The appeal of F. A. Harding provided its own drama and

the details of it reveal much of the General Conference's attitude toward slavery. However, it served only as a prelude to another more celebrated case, that of one of the bishops of the Methodist Episcopal Church, James O. Andrew.

On Monday, May 20, 1844, John A. Collins, of the Baltimore Conference, offered a resolution before the General Conference.

> Whereas it is currently reported, and generally understood, that one of the Bishops of the M. E. Church has become connected with slavery; and whereas it is due to this General Conference to have a proper understanding of the matter; therefore,
>
> Resolved, that the Committee on the Episcopacy be instructed to ascertain the facts in the case, and report the results of their investigation to this body tomorrow morning.[7]

On Wednesday morning, May 22, 1844, Bishop James O. Andrew presented a letter of facts to the Committee on the Episcopacy. Among these facts were (1) that an old lady of Augusta, Georgia, had bequeathed to Bishop Andrew a mulatto girl. He was to send the girl to Liberia when she reached the age of nineteen. When the time came, the girl refused to go. (2) About five years before, Bishop Andrew's mother-in-law left to her daughter a Negro boy. The laws of the state of Georgia, if not outright "ownership," prevented him from manumitting the boy. (3) In January of 1844, Bishop Andrew married a woman who possessed slaves. She was unwilling to hold the slaves and Bishop Andrew became the owner by deed of trust. Again, the laws of the state of Georgia did not permit Bishop Andrew to manumit these slaves.

Following Bishop Andrew's statement, a resolution was offered that referred to the position on slavery at the origin of the church: "and whereas it has been, from the origin of said Church, a settled policy and the invariable usage to elect no person to the office of Bishop who was embarrassed with this

great evil. . . ."[8] This resolution, offered by John Davis and
Alfred Griffith of the Baltimore Conference, left no room for
negotiation, quiet or otherwise. The resolution ended by
saying: "Resolved that the Rev. James O. Andrew be, and he
is hereby affectionately requested to resign his office as one of
the bishops of the Methodist Episcopal Church." The
resolution caused very deep feelings in the General
Conference. In addition to the resolution presented to the
General Conference by John A. Collins, of the Baltimore
Annual Conference, on Monday, May 20, 1844, another was
presented by John Davis and Alfred Griffith of the same
annual conference on Wednesday morning, May 22. The next
day James B. Findley of the Ohio Annual Conference offered
a substitute for the Davis and Griffith resolution. The
substitute referred to the long-standing rule on slavery in the
Book of Discipline of the Methodist Episcopal Church.
Findley's substitute ended by saying, "Resolved, that it is the
sense of this General Conference that he [Bishop Andrew]
desist from the exercise of his office so long as this
impediment [slave holding] remains."[9] The substitute was
signed by B. Findley and Joseph M. Trimble of the Ohio
Annual Conference. The substitute prevailed, 111 to 69,
another sure sign of division.

Even though the issue of slavery caused a sharp
confrontation, it was not the only issue of deep concern. The
Northern part of the Methodist Episcopal Church had a quite
different view of the office of a bishop than the Southern part
of the church. The North looked upon the office of bishop as
being an office of the General Conference. In this view a
bishop was accountable to the General Conference in a very
direct way.

The view of the South was that the office of bishop was a
separate and individual office. In this view, the bishop, once
he was elected by the General Conference, was then a
separate authority.

These two views of the episcopal office were in sharp conflict in the General Conference of 1844.

The suspension of Bishop Andrew stirred deep feelings in the Southern delegates. For some time they had felt the pressure from the abolitionists and a Northern majority. In fact, on June 3, 1844, William Capers of South Carolina, having sensed the divisive potential in the slavery issue, had proposed that there be two General Conferences. This was a forerunner of the jurisdictional structure which was yet to come.

Two days after Bishop Andrew was suspended, fifty-two delegates from the Southern Conferences presented a resolution. Some time later, a Plan of Separation was drawn up and presented to the General Conference. It was adopted by a vote of 135 to 15.

The Southern delegates proposed an organizational convention on May 1, 1845. One year later, on May 1, 1846, the first General Conference of the Methodist Episcopal Church, South, met in Peterburg, Virginia.

These two churches, so similar and yet so different, would remain apart for almost a century. They could only be reunited by a Plan of Union that would include the Central Jurisdiction. Slavery was succeeded by segregation.

The Road to Union

From the Great Separation in 1845 to Methodist Union in 1939, almost a century of mind-making was taking place. Historians of the period—and even later—looked upon the social institutions in the wider society as the norms for church life. There is abundant evidence that most church members and leaders did the same. In all of the long debates leading to union, few voices in the Methodist Episcopal Church, South, questioned the plans for a segregated structure.

During the negotiations leading to union, several proposals

were set forth, but all of the major ones recommended either a separate racial structure or an all–African American Methodist Church which the then-members of the church would be asked to join voluntarily. Just as slavery had been the determining factor in Methodist relations with African Americans, so also segregation had determined these relations during discussions on union. Joseph Allen makes the point clear when he writes, "Although slavery had vanished, racial segregation had taken its place, and union was impossible without agreement on the status of Negro members."[10]

There were other major concerns during the talks on Methodist union, but none received more attention than the question: "What shall be done about the black membership?"

Two proposals will illustrate this concern.

When the Commission on Union met in Cincinnati, Ohio, January 18-20, 1911, it considered several papers that had come to it. One paper, from the ministers and laymen in the Chattanooga, Tennessee, area, outlined plans for the African American membership. In its eighth point, the Chattanooga Proposal recommended:

> The Colored Methodists would best be served through a union of all the colored churches and members with the active financial and personal interests of the unified church. . . .
> If the union of all colored churches cannot be secured, try a plan for the union of the Colored Methodist Episcopal Church and the colored membership of the Methodist Episcopal Church. If that is not practicable, make another General Conference District for the colored membership, giving them the additional power to elect their bishops (with authority limited to their own district) and, as a fair offset, their delegates would not have voting power in the General Conference.[11]

Another example of the force of segregationist thinking during negotiations on union is this report from John M. Moore:

The South and the Southern Commissioners were all but unanimous in the opinion that a United Negro Methodist Church in the United States, embracing the Negro constituency in the Methodist Episcopal Church, the Colored Methodist Episcopal Church, and the two African Methodist Episcopal Churches, should be the goal in the union movement. To that end they held that the Negro membership of 315,000 in the Methodist Episcopal Church could best be served, and could best serve the cause of union, through an independent organization of their own.[12]

This pattern of thinking—that all African Americans would serve the church best by being all together—was quite prevalent in the early part of the twentieth century. What made this proposal so strange was its belief that racial union could be accomplished only on the basis of color with so little regard for other profound differences among African Americans in history and culture. There were other issues to be considered, some having nothing to do with race. But where race was considered, the segregationist pattern of thinking became clear.

The proposal for a "United Negro Methodist Church" was never in the minds of the African Methodist Episcopal or the African Methodist Episcopal Zion Churches. Having been formed because of segregation in the Methodist Episcopal Church, there was little or no chance that these two Methodist churches, now proud and independent, would give any thought to being segregated again.

One of the two African Americans on the Commission on Union of the Methodist Episcopal Church was Robert E. Jones. He was an outstanding leader, the editor of the *Southwestern Christian Advocate,* and a strong voice in racial matters. In a speech at Northwestern University in 1915, Jones said:

If the church draws the color line, then the preachers of hate and segregation will have gained a forceful endorsement of their propaganda which is as undemocratic, as un-American, as it is unchristian.[13]

Jones later became the first African American bishop to be elected (1920) for episcopal supervision over several black conferences in the United States.

The Fact of the Central Jurisdiction

If the General Conference of 1844 was dominated by the slavery issue, the Uniting General Conference of 1939 was filled with a spirit of hope for a new and, some said, glorious, era in the life of the church. In fact, Bishop John M. Moore described Methodist Union in this way:

> Methodist Union finally arrived after a very long hard journey. It started August 17, 1876, and came to a glorious destination on May 10, 1939, at 8:59 in the evening, a period of sixty-two years, eight months, and twenty-three days.[14]

There was little or no mention of the Central Jurisdiction in *The Daily Christian Advocate* of the 1939 Uniting Conference. Plans for the Central Jurisdiction were a part of the larger Plan of Union and this Plan had been hammered out and adopted earlier. All that was left to do now was to declare the union which had been discussed and agreed upon in earlier conferences and negotiations.

The Plan of Union, as it was declared on May 8, 1939, included one definitive sentence which described the Central Jurisdiction.

> Section VII   Boundaries
> ¶ 26 The Methodist Church in the United States of America shall have Jurisdictional Conferences made up as follows: . . .
>   Central—the Negro Annual Conferences, the Negro Mission Conferences and Missions in the United States of America.[15]

The Plan of Union had been adopted by a large margin of positive votes in the General Conferences of the Methodist Episcopal Church, the Methodist Protestant Church, and the Methodist Episcopal Church, South. For the Methodist Episcopal Church the vote was 470 for and 83 against, and for the Methodist Protestant Church, the vote was 142 for and 83 against. When the Plan of Union was presented to all of the annual conferences, the aggregate vote was 7,650 for and 1,247 against. Only one annual conference, North Mississippi, failed to accept the Plan of Union by a majority vote.[16]

The sentiment was quite different among African American delegates to the General Conference. Indeed, much earlier, upon hearing that a segregated structure would be proposed, several African American leaders spoke out against it. One of them, then a young pastor, Charles Carrington, wrote in 1936: "The plan violates the principle of brotherhood dominant in the life and teachings of Jesus and embodied in the organized fellowship of Christian believers in the Church."[17] James P. Brawley described the feelings of most African American delegates to the Uniting General Conference:

It was the hope of the Negro membership of the Methodist Episcopal Church that his status would be improved in the new United Church and that no structural organization would set him apart and give him less dignity and recognition than he already had. . . . He therefore rejected the Plan of Union. . . . This was a stigma too humiliating to accept.[18]

The rejection was decisive. Of the forty-seven African American delegates to the General Conference, thirty-six voted against the Plan of Union and eleven abstained. Brawley went on to say that when the General Conference rose to sing "We Are Marching to Zion," the African American delegates remained seated and some of them wept.[19]

If one asks why such a wide chasm existed between the heavy positive votes of white Methodists and the equally heavy negative votes of African Americans, the answer is to be found in the rejection of structural segregation on the part of African Americans.

Earlier Structures for African American Methodists

We have already seen how, from the beginning, Methodists expressed a strong interest in African Americans. During slavery this interest was expressed in many ways, one of them being the mission to the slaves.

The first Methodist structure for African Americans was the Mission Conference. As early as 1824, the General Conference had authorized colored preachers.

> The Annual Conference may employ colored preachers to travel and preach where their services are judged necessary: provided that no one shall be so employed without having been recommended according to the form of the Discipline.[20]

African American local churches needed preachers and their leaders reminded the General Conference of this in 1848. That General Conference did approve separate annual conferences for African American churches but voted nonconcurrence on independent churches within the Methodist Connectional System.

In 1864, the General Conference authorized the organization of African American Mission Conferences.

The first such conference to be organized was Delaware. It convened in Philadelphia, Pennsylvania in John Wesley Church (now Tindley Temple) on July 19, 1864. The conference was made up of the colored preachers and churches who preferred their own structuring for the work of the local churches. At the beginning, there were 21

preachers, 39 local preachers; 4,964 church members; 841
Sunday school scholars; and 34 churches.[21]

Once the movement of African American Mission Conferences started, it proceeded in the following order:

Washington Mission Conference, October 27, 1864
Mississippi Mission Conference, December 25, 1865
South Carolina Mission Conference, April 2, 1866
Tennessee Mission Conference, October 11, 1866
Texas Mission Conference, January 3, 1867
Georgia Mission Conference, October 10, 1867
North Carolina Mission Conference, January 14, 1868

These eight African American Mission Conferences, feeling the
first surge of energy, and some degree of independence, began
to act like annual conferences. But according to the rules under
which they were organized, these mission conferences (1) could
not send delegates to the General Conference; (2) could not
receive dividends from the Book Concern; and (3) could not
vote on Constitutional Amendments.[22]

Mindful of the latter two restrictions, but forgetful of the
first, these eight African American Mission Conferences
elected delegates to the General Conference of 1868. Faced
with a dilemma, the General Conference debated the matter
for ten days and then voted to rescind the rule against the
election of delegates from the Mission Conferences. By a vote
of 212 for and 14 against, the 1868 General Conference voted to
give the status of "Annual Conferences" to the Mission
Conferences and the two African American delegates were
seated.[23]

The first structure beyond the local church—mission
conferences—came after many appeals to the General
Conference; the second—annual conferences—came after a
personal presentation of a desire to be fully within the church,
according to the structural pattern of those days.

From 1868 to 1927, thirteen African American annual conferences were organized. These were:

> Mississippi Annual Conference, January 7, 1869
> Louisiana Annual Conference, January 13, 1869
> Lexington Annual Conference, March 2, 1869
> Florida Annual Conference, January 19, 1873
> West Texas, January 22, 1874
> Central Alabama, October 18, 1876
> Savannah, November 1, 1876
> Little Rock, February 21, 1879
> East Tennessee, October 25, 1880
> Central Missouri, March 24, 1887
> Upper Mississippi, February 5, 1891
> Atlanta, January 22, 1896
> South Florida, January 22, 1925

When the General Conference delegates from the Central Jurisdiction met during the Uniting Conference of 1939, they fixed the boundaries of the annual conferences of the Central Jurisdiction. Some of the annual conferences were compact, like the South Carolina Annual Conference. It was the largest of the nineteen, but its work was confined to the state of South Carolina. Other annual conferences extended over several states. One example is the Lexington Annual Conference.

Lexington Conference shall include the Negro work in the states of Kentucky, Ohio, Michigan, Indiana, Wisconsin, and Minnesota, except so much of the state of Illinois as is included in the Central West Conference, and except Whitley, Knox, Bell, and Harlan Counties in Kentucky.[24]

It was clear that, with one annual conference covering most of six states and another covering five, the Central Jurisdiction would not be very "central." In any case these nineteen annual conferences were those that came into The Methodist Church of 1939 and formed the Central Jurisdiction.

NOTES

1. *Journal of the General Conference of the Methodist Episcopal Church, 1840,* p. 134.
2. Ibid., p. 48.
3. Ibid., p. 59.
4. *Journal of the General Conference of the Methodist Episcopal Church, 1844,* p. 5.
5. *Doctrines and Disciplines of the Methodist Episcopal Church* (New York: G. Lane and C. B. Tippett, 1844), pp. 82-83.
6. *Journal of the General Conference, 1844,* p. 20.
7. Ibid., p. 58.
8. Ibid., p. 64.
9. Ibid., p. 66.
10. Joseph L. Allen, "The Methodist Union in the United States," in Nils Ehrenstrom and Walker G. Mueller, *Institution and Church Unity* (New York: Association Press, 1963), p. 284.
11. John M. Moore, *The Long Road to Methodist Union* (Nashville: Abingdon Press, 1943), p. 91.
12. Ibid., p. 137.
13. Robert E. Jones, "The Problem: The Negro," *A Working Conference on the Union of American Methodism,* p. 230.
14. Moore, *The Long Road to Methodist Union,* p. 23.
15. *Discipline of the Methodist Church* (New York: The Methodist Publishing House, 1940), The Plan of Union, para. 26, p. 28.
16. Moore, *The Long Road to Methodist Union,* p. 198.
17. Charles Carrington, "Methodist Union and the Negro," *The Crisis* May 1936, p. 158.
18. James P. Brawley, "Methodist Church from 1939," *Central Christian Advocate,* October 15, 1967, p. 3.
19. Ibid.
20. *Journal of the General Conference of the Methodist Episcopal Church, 1824,* vol. 1, p. 377.
21. John H. Graham, *Black United Methodists: Retrospect and Prospect* (New York: Vantage Press, 1979), p. 36.
22. Ibid., p. 40.
23. Ibid.
24. A Record of the Uniting Conference of the Methodist Episcopal Church, the Methodist Episcopal Church, South, and the Methodist Protestant Church, *The Daily Christian Advocate,* Tuesday, May 9, 1939, p. 365.

C H A P T E R 3

A Better
Chance?

A
mong the memorable dates in Methodist history,
two stand out as landmarks in the life of this
American denomination. The first is December 24,
1784 when the Christmas Conference convened in
Lovely Lane Chapel in Baltimore. The second is April 26,
1939—one hundred and fifty-five years later—when the
Uniting Conference convened in Kansas City, Missouri.

When the Christmas Conference convened, America, as a
nation of united states, was also being formed. When the
Uniting Conference convened, both the nation and the
church had celebrated a sesquicentennial celebration.
Although the century and a half of American Methodism had
seen many changes, attitudes on race were not among them.
After more than a third of the twentieth century had passed,
the legacy of the nineteenth century—so steeped in race, in
separation, in laws assuring the continuance of segregation—still governed much of the thinking in politics,
education, and even in religion.

Those who met in Kansas City, Missouri, for the Uniting
Conference of Methodism knew something of the high
significance of the occasion. In the episcopal address, the
Council of Bishops expressed its view of the Uniting
Conference:

> Methodism in America proclaims to the world today, with
> great joy, the culmination of one of the most outstanding and
> far-reaching movements which the Church of Christ has ever
> witnessed.[1]

48

The bishops took note of the Christmas Conference in 1784 and the General Conference of 1808 which "created an essential and elemental constitution in church government." They thought that the Uniting Conference was of that order. As they saw it, a new church was being formed in 1939, even though all of the parts of that new church had once belonged to the whole.

Trying to Find a New Way

On Tuesday, May 9, 1939, a committee chaired by Matthew Simpson Davage, an outstanding African American lay leader, reported to the Uniting Conference. Even though no African American delegate to the Uniting Conference voted for the Plan of Union, Dr. Davage knew that realism called for working within the Plan once it was adopted. In speaking for the Union, Dr. Davage said:

> I am for it. The proposed Plan of Unification . . . is not a perfect instrument—and . . . it does not wholly satisfy the desires of any single group. In making our decisions this day we are not called upon to agree that the thing proposed is perfect, but to decide whether or not this endeavor to bridge the gap between this ultimate ideal and the immediately possible reality is a step in the direction of one fold and one Shepherd. . . . Already the dawn heralding the beginning of a new day has appeared, a day of enlarged opportunity and of increased responsibility.[2]

It was this kind of faith in the future that led Matthew Davage to chair a Committee on Boundaries for a racial jurisdiction that was overwhelmingly rejected by his African American colleagues in the Uniting Conference.

The report of the Committee on Boundaries of the Central Jurisdiction included some Annual Conferences of a single state, such as Louisiana, some with two Annual Conferences in one state, such as Mississippi; and some Annual Conferences of several states, such as Lexington, Central West, and Delaware.

The original nineteen Annual Conferences forming the Central Jurisdiction included some that grew up from Mission Conferences in 1864 and Annual Conferences established later. The first to be organized was Delaware in 1864, as a Mission Conference; the last to be organized was the South Florida Annual Conference, organized by Bishop E. G. Richardson in Bradenton, Florida on January 22, 1925.[3]

When the Uniting Conference ended, there were three large groups of African Americans. First, there were those who remained with the northern branch of the former Methodist Episcopal Church. In this group were those found in the nineteen Annual Conferences that eventually formed the Central Jurisdiction. Then there were the African Methodist Episcopal and African Methodist Episcopal Zion Churches. Each of these separate denominations had churches in place where there were also Central Jurisdiction Churches. Then there were Colored Methodist Episcopal Churches that had formed a separate denomination in 1870.

Because of the strict separation of African Americans from other Methodists, these groups were often confused by white Methodists. Always resented by African Americans in the Central Jurisdiction, this ignorance sometimes touched vital interests, such as finance. And sometimes the confusion was sharpened by speeches that made color the chief characteristic by which white Methodists recognized African Americans, no matter what other distinctions they may have had.

An example of this occurred in the General Conference of 1940 when relationships were very fragile and future directions still quite unclear.

On April 30, 1940 the General Conference heard a report from its Committee on Special Days. Among other things, the Committee reported on Race Relations Sunday. This was the

definition as problems, why did so many African Americans remain in the Methodist Church? The answer was not often given in writing. It was expressed as a deep loyalty that raised other questions: why not stay in the church in which so many of them were born? Why not give racial inclusion relations a chance to prove itself to be workable in the church?

Those African Americans who remained in The Methodist Church did not always have a happy time. First, they had to hear the taunts that came from some leaders of independent black churches. Bishop Daniel A. Payne of the African Methodist Episcopal Church thought that African Americans in the Methodist Episcopal Church would always be in a minority status. He states it rather graphically: "The existence of the colored man in the M.E. Church, always was, still is, and ever must be a mere cipher."[6]

In spite of these taunts, there were, at the time of Methodist Union, approximately 300,000 African Americans in The Methodist Church. The few who did leave felt very deeply that their conscience would not allow them to serve in a church that was, by constitution, segregated. One of those was James Farmer, an outstanding Civil Rights leader, but before that, a Methodist from birth. Farmer explained his decision to leave the Methodist ministry by saying:

> The unification was a segregated one. There were to be six jurisdictions in the United Church—five of which were geographical, and the sixth, racial. A black church, whether in Portland, Oregon or in Chitterling Switch, Georgia, would be in the euphemistically named Central Jurisdiction. . . . How was I to preach Christ in a church whose structure gave him the lie?"[7]

But there was no mass exodus of African Americans from The Methodist Church, either before or after the Union.

Two reasons may account for the continuing membership of African Americans in The Methodist Church. The first was given by Willis J. King, a member of one of the Commissions on Union and later a bishop of the church:

> More important [to the Negro members], however, than rights and prerogatives was the instinctive conviction evident from their earliest connection with the people called "Methodists," that this fellowship represented a communion that was seriously seeking to build a brotherhood among all men. They believed that their membership in such a fellowship would help in the achievement of world brotherhood.[8]

The key words here are "instinctive conviction." Over 340,000 African American members believed that denominations of the white race only were not in accord with the best future of American race relations.

Another reason why so many African Americans remained in The Methodist Church was the vigor of the church's outreach to them, albeit within segregated structures. Missions to the slaves expressed interest in and care for the souls of slaves, even though these missions did nothing to change the institution of slavery. Then, just after the Civil War, Methodists were among the first to build schools and colleges for the education of the "freedmen."

Whatever their reasons for staying, the African Americans in The Methodist Church maintained a stubborn belief that the racial diversity of the church was important and that the Central Jurisdiction, though a high price for the union of the church, would not live forever.

Another way to view this phenomenon of the continuing presence of African American members in The Methodist Church is historical. If there were no mass defections in 1816 when the African Methodist Episcopal Church came into being, or in 1870 when the Colored Methodist Episcopal Church came into being, none could be expected in 1939 when the three largest branches of The Methodist Church in the United States came into being.

The Central Jurisdiction Conference: Its First Session

On June 18, 1940, at 9:00 A.M., the first session of the Central Jurisdictional Conference opened at Union Memorial Methodist Church in St. Louis. The first General Conference of The Methodist Church had convened two months earlier on April 24, 1940. By this time it was clear that the unification was a fact of life, with the jurisdictional structure firmly in place.

The membership of the Central Jurisdiction in 1940 was reported to be 344,671. There was abundant evidence of productive merit and activity among the nineteen Annual Conferences since the Declaration of Union in 1939. The work of the first Central Jurisdictional Conference was to be done in twenty committees, corresponding roughly to those that expressed the interests of the wider denomination of which the Central Jurisdiction was now a part.

The committees did the work assigned to them, as their reports indicated, but it quickly became clear that the major business of the Central Jurisdictional Conference would be the election of bishops. Official minutes of meetings rarely express deep feelings, but it must have been a tense moment when the first episcopal ballot was issued and counted on Thursday morning, June 20, 1940.

One hundred seventeen ballots were cast. Seventy-eight votes were necessary for election. On the first ballot, W. A. C. Hughes, then the secretary of Colored Work of the Board of Home Missions and Church Extension, received sixty-nine votes. On the second ballot Hughes received eighty-one votes and was declared elected. Thus began a new historical line of episcopal leadership for African Americans in The Methodist Church. Tragically, the first bishop elected to the Central Jurisdiction did not live to hold his first Annual Conference session. Bishop Hughes died within a month after his election.

On the morning of the fourth day of the Jurisdictional Conference, June 21, 1940, Lorenzo Houston King, the pastor of St. Mark's Church, New York City, was elected on ballot number five. Dr. King was a former editor of the *Southwestern Christian Advocate.* St. Mark's was an integral part of the New York Conference and did not belong to the Central Jurisdiction. The Central Jurisdiction made a statement by electing to the episcopacy a pastor who was a member of another jurisdiction.

The new bishops of the Central Jurisdiction faced a formidable task. With the death of Bishop Hughes, there had to be an apportionment of the work of the Central Jurisdiction among the three remaining bishops: Jones, Shaw, and King. Bishop Robert E. Jones, who was elected by the General Conference of 1920, was assigned to the Columbus (Ohio) Area; Bishop Alexander P. Shaw, elected by the General Conference of 1936, was assigned to the Baltimore Area. This area stretched from New York and New Jersey south to North Carolina and west through Tennessee. Bishop King was assigned to the Atlantic Coast Area, which included Georgia, Florida, Alabama, and South Carolina. The New Orleans Area, assigned earlier to Bishop Hughes, had to be reassigned after the bishop died.

Racially, the Central Jurisdiction was one close-knit unit. Geographically and sociologically it was wide-ranging in territory and cumbersome administratively. In most ways, the Central Jurisdiction was not central at all.

Sorting Things Out

As interesting as the geography of the Central Jurisdiction was, it was not in the same class as the dramas being played out in many places. These dramas centered around several questions that do not seem to be very important now, but were of great significance in 1940. Was the Central Jurisdiction to be regarded as an interim plan of union, as Willis J. King suggested? Or would the Central Jurisdiction become so convenient for white Methodists and so comfortable for African American Methodists that the pressure to include the jurisdiction in regional units would subside? No one could answer that question in 1940.

It should not be forgotten that there were a few prophetic voices who kept raising the question about the ethics of having a racial jurisdiction. Some of these voices came from the Central Jurisdiction; others from various parts of The Methodist Church. Dr. Lynn Harold Hough of Drew Theological Seminary said of the Central Jurisdiction: "In the face of this unanimous opposition by the Negro brethren and against what we so loudly profess as a Church, makes this a day of unutterable ignominy for the Methodist Episcopal Church."[9]

Nor did all of these prophetic voices come from the North. Walter Vernon reports that, as early as 1924, the Louisiana Annual Conference of the Methodist Episcopal Church voted in favor of the Union of the three Methodisms, but later disapproved of the plan to place black Methodists in a separate Central Jurisdiction.[10] This was all good for the record and perhaps did much to revive the hopes of many African American leaders, but the time was at hand to move ahead, and the Central Jurisdiction set about the task along with the other five regional jurisdictions of The Methodist Church.

As the Bishops Saw It

The Episcopal Address at the General Conference of 1940 took little note of the Plan of Union. There was no need to do so. The plan was many years in the making, and by 1940, it had been thoroughly discussed throughout the three uniting branches of Methodism. What was considered high priority now was to get on with the business of being a united church. When the bishops did come to a discussion of "Values Already Found in Union," they said:

> While the voting of the Negro Conferences indicated the feeling that the Plan of Union did not give to their people the recognition warranted by their achievements and worth, there has been among them a cordial acceptance of the outcome, with the growing conviction that under the new plan they have what may be called "a better chance."[11]

The bishops did not go on to explain what was meant by "a better chance." Perhaps they meant a better chance to develop leadership. In any event, they expected—and received—a loyal response from those who, having been represented in the church from its beginning, would remain now in the hope that fuller brotherhood and sisterhood could become a reality.

Unlike the Episcopal Address at the General Conference of 1940, the bishops of the Central Jurisdiction wrote a long section of their address on "The Central Jurisdiction." It was read by Bishop Robert E. Jones. Among other things, Bishop Jones and his colleagues said:

> After the Negro had registered his opinion and had been outvoted by a majority in the three churches, he logically and loyally submitted to the outcome. He did so with the sincerest and undivided purpose to make the very most of the situation.[12]

Then the bishops of the Central Jurisdiction quoted the Episcopal Address delivered to the white majority at the

General Conference. They, too, asked for "a better chance." It remained to be seen whether or not the two groups of bishops meant the same thing when they said "a better chance."

In the course of the Episcopal Address to the Central Jurisdictional Conference, the bishops did describe the "undertaking of interracial Christian brotherhood as the most notable experiment that has been essayed in the history of the Christian church."[13] This statement gave further strength to the belief that these leaders, now in a constitutional racial structure, did not see themselves fixed there forever. There would, to be sure, develop pockets of power and self-interest that would be content to stay intact for as many years as possible. But, after awhile, even these would have to yield to the "most notable experiment."

The bishops of the Central Jurisdiction struck two other notes that expressed their spirit in the first jurisdictional conference. The first was a note of pride and high resolve. They had no illusions about their position in the newly-united Methodist Church but there was little, if any, evidence of self-pity. Instead, the bishops wrote:

> We are expected to stand upon our feet, with our heads up, our eyes in front of our heads, our chests expanded, and our shoulders back, and to make like men and women who are soldiers of Christ in everything.[14]

Then, to underscore the importance of such a spirit, the bishops said:

> This Jurisdictional Conference does give us an opportunity to show the stuff of which we are made.[15]

Before the Jurisdictional Conference adjourned, there was strong evidence that the episcopal leaders of the Central Jurisdiction would not easily accept anything less than the best that could be given by the members of the local churches of their far-flung areas.

The second note that was struck by the bishops of the Central Jurisdiction was one of further African American church union. They invited African American Christians of other independent branches of Methodism to join those now in the Central Jurisdiction. They said:

It is evident that we are going to be compared by the best standards of the world. . . . We would have no other standards and if for any reason we do not measure up to the last notch, but make a reasonably fair average in the grading of our own conduct, we ought to be happy, take courage and move forward and our friends will thereby have every reason for rejoicing.

In this connection it seems consistent that we would welcome into the Central Jurisdiction any of the distinctive Negro bodies if they so desire, especially the Colored Methodist Episcopal Church, provided the General Church extends the invitation and provided further, of course, that the plan as set up proves agreeable to them and to us.[16]

In the atmosphere of 1940, this was a radical suggestion. A larger structure for African American Methodists was considered during the long discussions on Union but this was done from the motive of freeing the church of "the Negro problem."

At a meeting in Savannah, Georgia, January 23 to February 6, 1918, the Committee of the Status of the Negro Membership presented a report. It was a time when the Joint Commission on Union was considering the possibility of Associate Regional Conferences. The Committee reported as follows:

Your committee have found it impossible to present their conclusions as to what should be the status of the Negro membership in the reorganized and unified Church without stating the same in a form which relates this subject to questions already reported upon by coordinate committees and tentatively adopted by the Joint Commission.[17]

Then the report went on to say:

We present, as a preferential report the following, which places the Negro membership in an Associate Regional Jurisdiction of the kind and with the powers herein indicated.[18]

Later, an alternative report was presented which "places the Negro membership in an Associate General Conference which shall comprise within its jurisdiction the Negro membership of the Church in the United States and Africa."[19]

When the invitation offered by the Central Jurisdiction to the independent branches is seen against this background, several interesting questions arise. What was the difference between the invitation from the Central Jurisdiction and this earlier one from the report quoted above? The earlier report invites all African Americans *out* to form a giant racial church. The other, from the Central Jurisdiction, invites these black denominations *into* what, it was hoped, would be an interracial fellowship of Methodists. The difference is vast.

There were other questions along the way. How could the African Methodist Episcopal Church, which was organized in 1816, almost thirty years before the division of The Methodist Church, be expected to come back into a denomination that segregated its founder and was still segregating other African Americans again one hundred and twenty-three years later? And how could the Colored Methodist Episcopal Church, with seventy years of living as a mature independent Methodist denomination, be expected to leave that heritage for a larger black unity in the segregated Methodist Church? For the Central Jurisdiction and for the larger Methodism to which it belonged there were many questions to be answered in 1940.

One question that was at first overlooked and then later reconsidered was the status of the church in Liberia. In earlier reports, it was recommended that Liberia become a part of the Central Jurisdiction. The Plan of Union contained no such provision. However, on June 22, 1940, L. S. Moore, Chairman of the Committee on Boundaries of the Central Jurisdiction, presented a memorial asking that the General Conference enact a constitutional revision to place the Liberian Annual Conference with the Central Jurisdiction. The General Conference of 1944 considered this matter favorably and Liberia became a part of the Central Jurisdiction, remaining in this relationship for twenty years. With the election of the first Liberian bishop in 1944, Liberia became a Central Conference of The Methodist Church.

NOTES

1. *Journal of the Uniting Conference*, The Methodist Church, 1939, p. 148.
2. Methodist Episcopal Church, General Conference, *The Daily Christian Advocate*, May 5, 1936, p. 88.
3. John H. Graham, *Black United Methodists: Retrospect and Prospect* (New York: Vantage Press, 1979), p. 46.
4. General Conference of 1940, *The Daily Christian Advocate*, April 30, 1940, p. 151.
5. Ibid., p. 152.
6. Daniel A. Payne, *History of the African Methodist Episcopal Church* (Salem, N.H.: Ayer Publishing Co., 1969), p. 10.
7. James Farmer, *Lay Bare the Heart* (New York: New American Library, 1985), p. 143.
8. Willis J. King, "The Negro in Methodism: 1939," in the *Central Christian Advocate*, October 1, 1967, p. 7.
9. *Central Christian Advocate*, vol. 142, no. 2, January 15, 1967, p. 6.
10. Walter N. Vernon, *Becoming One People* (Bossier City, La: The Everett Publishing Co., 1987), p. 231.
11. General Conference, 1940, *The Daily Christian Advocate*, April 30, 1940, p. 41.
12. *Journal of the Central Jurisdictional Conference* 1940, p. 54.
13. Ibid., p. 57.
14. Ibid., p. 58.
15. Ibid.
16. Ibid., p. 59.
17. See John M. Moore, *The Long Road to Methodist Union* (Nashville: Abingdon Press, 1943), p. 138.
18. Ibid.
19. *Journal of the Central Jurisdictional Conference*, 1940, p. 100.

A Standard
Second to None

There was very little mention of the Central Jurisdiction in the Episcopal Address of 1944. However, the unavoidable issue of race came before the General Conference and it was addressed also in several Jurisdictional Conferences. When America was involved heavily in a war against the super-race ideas of Adolf Hitler, it was impossible to move past the racial issue in the United States of America.

At the General Conference of 1944, the bishops addressed the elected members on "Achievements of Methodist Union." Later in the address, the bishops wrote about "The World in Which We Must Live." Then they went on to the "Assertion of the Christian Conscience." Under this heading, the bishops discussed several problems, one of them being "The Problem of Race." They began by saying: "Racial antagonism always creates a stubborn problem for the Christian religion because it stoutly resists the universal propagation of the Christian message and denies the doctrine of the brotherhood of man."[1]

The bishops did not make any connection between this statement on race and the existence of the Central Jurisdiction. However, they did go on to say:

In this country a minority group of thirteen million Negroes is compelled to remain a detached racial unit, is accorded a sub-Christian status, is given an uncertain standard of livelihood, and all the artificial standards which arise from racial grouping.[2]

This reference to racial grouping was not applied to the Central Jurisdiction. The tone of the address, and the intent to speak of race in broad international terms, precluded a reference to a matter that was considered settled, at least for a long time. Near the conclusion, the Episcopal Address did commit the bishops and General Conference to find a better way in race relations.

We make our own declaration of one who long ago has been the prophet of the better day in race relations: "In the name and spirit of science and education we will seek to find and tell the truth. In the name and Spirit and of democracy we will seek the way of equal opportunity."[3]

This appeal to the Christian conscience would not be forgotten by those who did make specific references. But 1944 was a time of preoccupation with the mission of the church in a world at war and in need of great missionary outreach.

One who did make a pointed reference to segregation was a young minister who spoke to the Southeastern Jurisdictional Conference on Saturday evening, June 24, 1944. The Reverend Mr. George Wesley Jones was speaking primarily to young people, but his address was also aimed at the entire conference. When he came to the section of his address, "Racialism," he said: "The first of these (obstacles) is Racialism, which is an outright denial of the basic laws of the Kingdom, for it certainly seems to deny the fatherhood of God and refuses to exercise the love of one's neighbor."[4]

Then he went on to describe a train ride from Columbus, Ohio, where he sat across from a young Negro student with whom he had shared friendship all week at a Youth Conference. Mr. Jones went on to say that, when the train passed an imaginary geographical line, the Negro student had to go back to another coach. "Our fellowship was broken, and though I knew it would happen, I was hurt, and I was made more than ever aware of the impossibility of establishing the Kingdom until this sort of evil, this racialism is wiped away."[5] These, and other statements like them, were uttered as a witness to the ideal in Christian race relations. They would become a part of the yeast that would produce later statements and actions aimed at improved race relations.

Even though there was little contact between leaders of the Central and other jurisdictions in 1944, there were some occasions when such joint fellowship was very important. The 1944 Southeastern Jurisdictional Conference met in Atlanta, Georgia. There were two Methodist bishops resident in Atlanta, Bishop Arthur J. Moore of the Southeastern Jurisdiction and Bishop Lorenzo H. King of the Central Jurisdiction. Bishop King was invited to bring greetings to the Southeastern Jurisdictional Conference. He did so briefly and then presented his newly elected colleague, Bishop Willis J. King to speak.

When Bishop Lorenzo King spoke, he said:

I understand that you have taken a special action recently in this session to set up a committee that is to explore this whole matter of our interracial relations in the area of the Christian Church. I want to commend that. You know it is a forward step. I believe it is divinely inspired, and I trust that you will follow that through to what we anticipate will be a far-reaching and happy conclusion.[6]

When Bishop Willis J. King arose to speak, he referred to the newness of the jurisdictional system and the mutual difficulty of making adjustments. He went on to say:

We appreciate very much this courtesy, the beautiful courtesy we think you are showing to us in presenting us at this time. . . . We have been made to feel that we, like you, are Methodists, and that fine phrase that Brother Garber,

now Bishop Garber, gave us some years ago makes us realize
again that the Methodists were one people.[7]

At this point, it was clear that the heavy negative vote against
the Plan of Union was not left in the past, as a matter of
history, and would not continue to be a point of debate after
just one quadrennium of experience with the jurisdictional
system. Bishop Willis J. King recognized this when, later in
his address, he said:

> We appreciate further the fact that you are struggling with a
> problem which we down here in the South can't get away
> from, if we would, and that you are trying to find, as we are,
> your way to the light.
>   At the same time we are all struggling with this new
> machinery, the Jurisdictional Conference.[8]

All of the bishops recognized that race was not the only reason
for establishing jurisdictional conferences. They also recognized that race was high on the list of any other reasons that
were set forth.

While the Episcopal Address at the Central Jurisdictional
Conference of 1944 was entitled "Message of the College of
Bishops," it could well have been called "A Statement of
Pride." Just after acknowledging that "We entered the work
of the new quadrennium in 1940. . . with many forebodings
and much uncertainty," the bishops went on to spell out what
they meant and how they felt.

> It [the Central Jurisdiction] was an administrative arrange-
> ment against which a majority of us had voted. Having been
> loyal Methodists, we accepted the mandate of the majority in
> the Church and set about our work determined to succeed
> and make the quality of the service rendered by our
> Jurisdiction second to none among the jurisdictions of our
> American Methodism.[9]

"Second to none"—it was a phrase that was heard often by my college generation (1935–39). It was repeated even more often during the quadrennium of 1940–44. The pride of African Americans, so long overlooked by those who were preoccupied with segregation, had come to the forefront. Long before the term "black pride" had become popular, the reality of Negro pride was writ large in African American literature and organizations, including the church.

Messages from the World

Even though the white press seemed to be startled by the "new" African American militance of the 1940s, it was never really new nor was it very radical. As African Americans saw it, over eighty years had passed since the Emancipation Proclamation. The militance of the forties, they felt, could only be new to those who did not share the inner life of African American people and it could only be radical if one focused on the "impertinence" of those few who would challenge long-standing practices of segregation which, by then, had the momentum of time behind them.

The bishops of the Central Jurisdiction were well aware of this "new" mood among African Americans. This is the way they saw the Central Jurisdiction at that time:

> We are not at all in harmony with any Methodists or others who think such a plan necessary in a truly Christian brotherhood. We consider it expedient only on account of the Christian childhood of some Methodists who need a little coddling until they grow into full grown manhood and womanhood in Christ Jesus. We are hopeful that in the near future our Methodism may become sufficiently Christian in character and maturity to find a more excellent way.[10]

When the bishops referred to the Christian childhood of many Methodists who voted for the Central Jurisdiction, they were not overdrawing their view of the world of the 1940s.

As early as 1933, the NAACP had filed suit against the University of North Carolina on behalf of Thomas Hocutt, a would-be student. The case was lost on a technicality, but it signaled the dawning of a new day in American race relations.[11] Within two years, another suit was filed, again in higher education. Later, in 1936, the NAACP filed suit in a campaign to equalize teachers' salaries in Montgomery County, Maryland. Then, in 1937, the Supreme Court ruled that the state of Maryland must provide equal educational opportunities and facilities within its boundaries for an African American student, Lloyd Gaines.

If the church were sealed off from the major social movements in society, one might have expected less militance on the part of its African American members. But the church was very often the place where many African Americans received both vision and direction for the task of liberation in society.

By 1941, one hundred thousand African Americans had threatened to march on Washington, against the protests of President Franklin Delano Roosevelt, to support fair employment in the war industries. The President eventually issued Executive Order 8802, which forbade racial and religious discrimination in war industries. The next day, A. Philip Randolph called off the march.

By the time the Central Jurisdictional Conference met in Greensboro, North Carolina in 1944, the pressure in race relations had reached a dangerous point. White and African American soldiers had fought in a series of racial incidents. Members of the Central Jurisdiction were keenly aware of these events, both in 1940 and in 1944. Because World War II demanded a strong verbal commitment to democratic principles, any practice of segregation became all the more glaring. Church members were determined that the actual practice of good race relations would become at least as visible in the church as they were in other sectors of society.

That is why the Central Jurisdictional Episcopal Address of 1944 expressed two very strong points of view. The first was for the Central Jurisdiction to get on with the business at hand. The bishops of the Central Jurisdiction meant no overstatement when they said that they would "set about our work determined to succeed." The second theme of the Episcopal Address at the 1944 Central Jurisdictional Conference was a protest, albeit a dignified one, of the segregation which, at that late date, seemed very much out of place in the church. That is why the bishops could say that "we are not at all in harmony with Methodists or others who think such a plan necessary in a truly Christian brotherhood."

The Episcopal Address delivered at the 1944 Central Jurisdictional Conference underscored a sense of pride. The bishops said: "Never before in our history has the general morale of our people been better."[12] Also:

> We believe in a Christian Social order which actually practices respect for human personality without discrimination; that allows all men freedom of opportunity, freedom of speech if what they say is worth speaking, freedom from want and freedom from fear and intimidation.[13]

The pride of the Central Jurisdiction in 1944 was further expressed in what was expected of its institutions:

> . . . we recommend and call upon our Board of Education and Methodism generally to raise all of the educational institutions recognized as colleges, junior colleges or high schools to the A grade standard by the agencies that have charge of the rating of educational institutions.[14]

And, concerning an adequate ministry: "They must be at least the equals in quality and efficiency of those in other professions and avocations which they will be expected to lead."[15]

From beginning to end, this episcopal address set forth and appealed to the pride of the members and leaders of the Central Jurisdiction.

The Pride Extends to Africa

On June 22, 1940, the chairman of the Committee on Boundaries of the Central Jurisdictional Conference made his report. The first report contains one item: a memorial asking that "the Central Jurisdiction Conference memorialize the General Conference to enact such constitutional revision as will place the Liberian Annual Conference in the Central Jurisdiction."[16] This motion was seconded and adopted with little or no debate.

There is no evidence to suggest that this motion came from any motive other than a serious concern to continue the mission of The Methodist Church in Liberia. Since 1833, the church had been at work through missionaries to Liberia. And, as early as 1858, the General Conference had shown its concern by electing African American missionary bishops. The first of these was Francis Burns, elected in 1858. He was followed by J. W. Roberts, elected in 1866; Isaac Scott, elected in 1904; and Alexander P. Camphor, elected in 1916. Now, since the Central Jurisdiction was already spread over the forty-eight United States, and since it was clearly based on color, this memorial seemed to fit the logic of race, if not geography.

The General Conference of 1944 must have acted favorably upon the memorial. On the second day of the Second Central Jurisdictional Conference, Dr. Matthew Simpson Davage of the Louisiana Conference moved that "we proceed to elect the bishop for Liberia first!"[17] The motion prevailed and Willis

J. King, then the president of Gammon Theological Seminary in Atlanta, was elected on the first ballot.

Other Episcopal Elections

Since the election of a bishop for Liberia was a special election, it was not counted among the others to be taken for general superintendent. On ballot number one of the regular election, none of the twenty-eight persons receiving votes had a number sufficient for election. There was no election on ballot number two. On ballot number three, Robert N. Brooks, then the editor of the *Central Christian Advocate*, was elected as a fourth bishop of the Central Jurisdiction, which now included Liberia. On ballot number five, Edward W. Kelly, then the pastor of Union Memorial Church in St. Louis, was elected.

When the chairman of the subcommittee on episcopal assignment made his report, Bishop Lorenzo H. King was assigned to the Atlantic Coast Area; Bishop Alexander P. Shaw to the Baltimore Area; Bishop Edward W. Kelly was assigned to the Columbus Area; Bishop Robert N. Brooks to the New Orleans Area; and Bishop Willis J. King to the Monrovia, Liberia Area.

After twenty-four years of service, Bishop Robert E. Jones was retired. The death of Bishop Matthew W. Clair was announced. Within five years, another new era in episcopal leadership had begun.

The first two African American bishops elected for service in the United States had now moved from the scene of active episcopal leaders. Robert E. Jones and Matthew W. Clair, elected in Des Moines, Iowa, at the General Conference of 1920, had been the symbols of pride in African American church circles for almost a quarter of a century. They had served during a most difficult time in American church history. Elected at the end of World War I, they had served up to and during World War II. Now a new era was taking shape as the Central Jurisdiction completed the election of its fifth bishop.

Pride in Stewardship

Feeling keenly the urgency of needs created by World War II, the General Conference of 1944 approved a Quadrennial Emphasis called the Crusade for Christ. It was a crusade for a new world order. It included major emphases upon evangelistic preaching, stewardship, and church school revitalization.

As a part of a world-wide relief program, the General Conference approved a goal of $25 million. This money was to be used for reconstruction and to help meet some of the dire needs created by the war.

All of the six jurisdictions stretched themselves to meet the overall goal of $25 million. The Central Jurisdiction was apportioned $796,300. With its best efforts put forward, the Jurisdiction raised $770,330.37. But the first episcopal area to pay its quota in full was one from the Central Jurisdiction. The New Orleans Area had an apportionment of $223,375. It actually paid $227,249.50. And it did this within a year after the General Conference adopted the overall goal. Six other Central Jurisdiction conferences paid their quotas in full. These were Atlanta, Central Alabama, Delaware, Florida, North Carolina, and South Carolina.[18]

Years That End in Four

Near the beginning of their Episcopal Address to the General Conference of 1944, the bishops found some significance in the fact that: "The forty-fourth year in each of the three last centuries has played a decisive role in the history of Methodism."[19] They referred to June 1744, when the first Methodist Conference convened in the Foundry in London. Then in 1844, that fateful General Conference was held that saw the division of the church, North and South. The year 1944 was the bicentennial of the first Methodist Conference and the centenary of the unhappy division. For the Central Jurisdiction, the year 1944 represented a time of "showing the stuff of which we are made." Having expressed its mind about the jurisdiction, and having worked together for four years, the Second Central Jurisdictional Conference set about achieving a record that was second to none in the church.

NOTES

1. Proceedings of the Second General Conference of the Methodist Church, *The Daily Christian Advocate*, April 27, 1944, p. 27.
2. Ibid., p. 27.
3. Ibid., p. 29.
4. Proceedings of the Second Southeastern Jurisdictional Conference, *The Daily Christian Advocate*, Tuesday, June 27, 1944, p. 101.
5. Ibid.
6. Ibid., p. 115.
7. Ibid.
8. Ibid.
9. *Journal of the Central Jurisdictional Conference*, 1944, p. 52.
10. Ibid.
11. See Lerone Bennett, Jr., *Before the Mayflower* (Baltimore: Penguin Books, 1966), p. 393.
12. *Journal of the Central Jurisdictional Conference*, 1944, p. 53.
13. Ibid.
14. Ibid., p. 57.
15. Ibid., p. 58.
16. *Journal of the Central Jurisdictional Conference*, 1940, p. 100.
17. *Journal of the Central Jurisdictional Conference*, 1944, p. 77. See also John H. Graham, *Black United Methodists Retrospect and Prospect* (New York: Vantage Press, 1979) p. 93.
18. Proceedings of the Second Annual Conference of the Methodist Church 1944, *The Daily Christian Advocate*, April 27, 1944, p. 17.
19. Ibid.

A Beginning
of Study

The year 1948 was an unusual one in many ways. For one thing, it was the year when the Crusade for Christ ended. This quadrennial program, which began in 1944, was aimed primarily at the recovery of Europe, whose suffering during World War II was deep and long-lasting. In the Episcopal Address of 1948, it was reported that the Methodist people had overpaid the goal of $25 million by contributing $27,011,243.

At the General Conference, the bishops made no mention of the jurisdictional system in general, nor of the Central Jurisdiction in particular. In two quadrennia of work all jurisdictions, including the Central Jurisdiction, had found a way of working in a new structure. New and larger concerns of international dimensions had taken over the headlines.

Even though the Episcopal Address made no mention of the Central Jurisdiction, it did underscore Methodism's commitment to the equality of all persons in the sight of God. Bishop G. Bromley Oxnam, who read the address, said, for all of the bishops: "Methodism is determined to preach a Gospel that insists that all men are brothers and children of one Father, to whom loyalty is due!"[1]

This statement appeared in a section on "The Freedom of the Methodist Pulpit." It probably had reference to the difficulty in preaching on race relations during a time when African Americans began to challenge the very foundations of segregation.

However silent the Episcopal Address may have seemed to be, the bishops were quite aware of some of the events that were taking place in the wider society. On April 9, 1947, the Congress on Racial Equality sent its first "Freedom Rider" group through the South. Then on April 10, Branch Rickey, who happened to be Methodist, opened the way for Jackie Robinson to join the Brooklyn Dodgers baseball team. Robinson would become the first African American in organized baseball in modern times. It became clear that segregation in all of its forms, was being attacked and that any racial structure, whether of church or of state, would be open to that attack.

This note was sounded in the General Conference of 1948 by a fraternal delegate from the African Methodist Episcopal Church. Speaking to the General Conference on April 30, 1948, Dr. G. Wayman Blakely expressed the historic indebtedness of the African Methodist Episcopal Church to world Methodism. Then he went on to say:

> For example, he (a Negro) begins his ride upon the train in the morning a first-class citizen and ends his journey behind the curtains as a second-rate untouchable. But being unwilling to sell his birthright for a mess of communistic pottage, he contemplates his future.[2]

These statements condemned segregation in general, but it was easy to see their implications for the Central Jurisdiction.

Earlier Proposals for Study

As early as 1944, the General Conference saw the dilemma of the Central Jurisdiction and sought ways to end it. In 1944, the General Conference had declared: "We look to the ultimate elimination of racial discrimination in The Methodist Church." It appointed a study committee to "consider afresh the relations of all races included in the membership of The Methodist Church and report back to the 1948 General Conference."[3] When the report was made in 1948, it was referred to boards and agencies for systematic study and use in activities and publications.

It was in this year, 1948, that the Central Jurisdiction decided on a study of itself. On Saturday, June 12, 1948, Dr. James P. Brawley, the president of Clark College in Atlanta, Georgia, "moved that a commission be appointed by the College of Bishops to study the Central Jurisdiction during the quadrennium 1948–52."[4] It was appointed.

The full motion authorizing the Commission read as follows:

> Commission to Study the Central Jurisdiction Motion: that the Central Jurisdiction authorize the setting up of a special commission to study the Central Jurisdiction during the quadrennium of 1948–1952, with the following personnel: The College of Bishops of the Central Jurisdiction, two ministers, two laymen from each area of the Central Jurisdiction, the senior bishop of the Jurisdiction to be the convenor. Amendment: with power to report to the General Conference in 1952.
>
> *Purpose*
>
> The purpose of this Commission shall be to study the Central Jurisdiction with a view to determining its advantages and its disadvantages; its relationship to other Jurisdictions; its overlapping boundaries; problems arising out of its extensive geography; its status as a racial group in the Methodist Church; and any other problems peculiar to the Jurisdiction. This study shall have as its purpose the establishment of an intelligent basis for determining whether or not the Central Jurisdiction should be continued as it now exists or eliminated, and what modifications, if any, should be made, and the steps necessary to make such modifications.
>
> James Brawley[5]

There are at least two significant points about this action. First, it is an extensive motion, indicating the firm intention to study all aspects of the Central Jurisdiction. Second, the amendment to the motion gives the Commission the power to report to the General Conference. This is the first clear intention of the Central Jurisdiction to be a vital part of solving the dilemma of race in The Methodist Church.

Just as the Episcopal Address to the General Conference was silent on the issue of the Central Jurisdiction, so also were the bishops of the Central Jurisdiction in placing their emphasis upon other matters. Both addresses emphasized the Crusade for Christ, both talked about the world in which the church lived, both pointed to the future.

Such references as were made to the Central Jurisdiction by its bishops were aimed at responsibility and achievement. The Episcopal Address to the Central Jurisdiction noted that of the $73,707 given by the total Methodist Church on Race Relations Sunday in 1944, the Central Jurisdiction had given $27,028 or 36 percent. Since this offering was for the support of the twelve African American colleges of the church, this was a significant achievement.

The Episcopal Address to the Central Jurisdiction also stressed the growth in leadership. The bishops said:

> In 1944 there were only three full-time Executive Secretaries [a term used to define directors of Christian education] in the nineteen Annual Conferences. The other five Conferences have either part-time or no volunteer workers. The Church has long since realized that a Conference Executive Secretary is a first step toward a vital and effective program of Christian training.[6]

While there was no mention of the Central Jurisdiction as a racial unit, the bishops did call for more loyalty and larger effort from its people.

> This Central Jurisdictional Conference must challenge our people to a more vigorous and better supported program. This one thing we must do. With our faces set steadfastly

toward the future we must honestly try to make decisions that will hasten the full expression of Christian ideals in our total personal and social life.[7]

The Episcopal Address to the Central Jurisdiction made strong reference to two issues: (1) Civil rights, and (2) the Jurisdictional System concerning civil rights. It said:

Any unfairness or mistreatment of any racial, religious or national group is a matter of concern to all those peoples as well as to us. We cannot escape the fact that our civil rights record has been an issue in world politics.[8]

An even sharper word was said on the jurisdictional system:

We probably do not need to add a paragraph on the jurisdictional system which is one of those children's diseases which Methodism, if it is ever to become a healthy denomination, must outgrow.[9]

Perhaps this brief statement expressed quite clearly what earlier Episcopal Addresses had said in a full section or in paragraphs.

The Third Central Jurisdictional Conference

On Wednesday, June 9, 1948, the third Central Jurisdictional Conference convened in Atlanta, Georgia. Special attention was given to the interests of Africa. Bishop Willis J. King, who had spent four years in Liberia, spoke and made a plea for more Christian workers to join him in Africa. He was followed by Bishop Robert N. Brooks who said:

The salvation of Africa is not to be determined by sending missionaries to Africa, but it is to be saved by beginning a steady stream of students from there coming into our

American colleges, where they can be trained and return to Africa, to lift their own people.[10]

Bishop Arthur J. Moore, of the Southeastern Jurisdiction, visited the Conference and spoke. Dr. W. F. Quillian, the Executive Secretary of the Southeastern Jurisdictional Conference was also introduced and brought greetings.

The major business of this Jurisdictional Conference was its committee work and the election of a bishop. On the third ballot, J. W. E. Bowen, then the editor of the *Central Christian Advocate*, was elected as the sixth bishop of the Central Jurisdiction.

Another item of civil rights interest came on Friday, June 11, 1948. After an address by Dr. Channing H. Tobias, a member of President Truman's Civil Rights Committee, Charles H. Dubra of Mississippi offered a resolution approving the proposals of that Committee. Edgar A. Love of the Washington Conference offered an amendment. His amendment requested that President Truman issue an executive order abolishing segregation in the armed forces. This was another indication of how members of the Central Jurisdiction felt about segregation in general and about a segregated structure in particular.

Continuing the theme of making a record second to none, the Committee on Education proposed, at the beginning of its report,

> that we reexamine the policies underlying our system of higher educational institutions in the Central Jurisdiction to the end that the general administration, the relationship and effectiveness of the system as a whole may be strengthened.[11]

These references underscored the intention of the leaders of the Central Jurisdiction to keep its institutions strong as long as the jurisdiction existed.

The Central Jurisdiction in 1952

If the 1948 Episcopal Address to the General Conference was silent on the issue of the Central Jurisdiction, the address of 1952 faced the issue squarely and without reserve. Writing under a section entitled "The Negro in the Methodist Church in the United States," the bishops outlined the progress that had been made by the Negro in America since the days of emancipation. Their conclusion was that:

> To discriminate against a person solely upon the basis of his race is both unfair and unChristian. Every child of God is entitled to that place in society which he has won by his industry, his integrity, and his character. To deny him that position of honor because of the accident of his birth is neither honest democracy nor good religion.[12]

This was, by far, the most forthright statement made by the bishops since the beginning of the Central Jurisdiction. And it is quite significant that the author of the Episcopal Address was a bishop of the South, Bishop Paul Kern.

The Episcopal Address also faced up to the specific issue of the Central Jurisdiction more squarely than any other up to that time. For the first time in a General Conference the different alternatives for dealing with the jurisdictions were mentioned. The bishops felt that

> a) Some would stabilize the situation upon the basis of the present pattern, urging an enlarged effort to increase the effectiveness of the Central Jurisdiction. . . . b) Others would do away with the Central Jurisdiction. c) Still others would abandon the jurisdictional system altogether. d) The General Conference could, by majority action, allow any existing jurisdiction to change its boundaries and, upon concurrence of the Negro Annual Conferences within that jurisdictional area, to merge all the annual conferences within that territory into one jurisdiction.[13]

Having laid out the alternatives so clearly, the Episcopal Address made it virtually impossible for any future General Conference to remain silent on the issue of the Central Jurisdiction. Also, for the first time, a note was introduced into this Episcopal Address that had been in no other since unification.

> Would we not be more likely to find a happier and more Christian solution to these questions if we approached them not from the standpoint of problems but from the standpoint of opportunities? Our failures are grist for the propaganda mills of our critics and enemies.[14]

This is the first time that the idea of thinking of the Central Jurisdiction as an opportunity was ever presented to a General Conference.

The Central Jurisdiction Speaks

The Fourth Central Jurisdictional Conference of The Methodist Church convened in Tindley Temple Methodist Church on Wednesday, June 18, 1952. In one of its early actions, the Conference set the time of Friday morning for hearing the report of the Commission to Study the Central Jurisdiction.[15] In another action, the Conference heard a statement from Dr. W. N. Ross of the Liberia Annual Conference. Dr. Ross's statement was a set of resolutions requesting the Central Jurisdictional Conference to approve the request of the Liberia Conference to be admitted to the Central Jurisdiction. It was voted to consider the resolution.

Turning to the major business of the Jurisdictional Conference, ballots were cast for two bishops on Thursday morning, June 20, 1952. The report of the first ballot revealed a wide spread of voting, for twenty-four persons, with Edgar A. Love and Matthew W. Clair receiving the largest number of votes. With seventy-eight votes necessary for election, Love received fifty-two votes and Clair thirty-eight.

On the second ballot, Love received sixty-four votes and Clair fifty-one. Results of the third ballot showed the election of Love. And on the fourth ballot, Clair was elected with 84 of the 116 votes cast. With the election of Edgar A. Love and Matthew W. Clair the Central Jurisdiction consecrated its seventh and eighth bishops.

Report of the Commission to Study the Jurisdiction

When James P. Brawley made the report of the Commission to study the Central Jurisdiction, there was considerable discussion. The report was adopted and the Commission continued for another quadrennium. There was additional discussion about the personnel of the continuing commission. C. Anderson Davis moved that the Commission be composed of two members from each annual conference. This amendment was not adopted. James P. Brawley made a substitute motion that the composition of the Commission "shall be the College of Bishops of the Central Jurisdiction, two ministers and two laymen from each Area of the Jurisdiction." This substitute prevailed.

The two episcopal addresses—to the General Conference and to the Central Jurisdictional Conference—gave specific attention to the Central Jurisdiction. The bishops of the Central Jurisdiction still looked upon the Central Jurisdiction as an experiment. They wrote: "The Methodist Church is an experiment in pan-racialism. Within it are all the races of the world. It is not a biracial church. It is a pan-racial church and the Negro is only one of the many races that compose it."[16]

But this statement did not diminish the concern that the bishops had for a segregated structure. After writing about the pan-racialism of The Methodist Church, they went on to say:

The church should allow complete freedom of choice to individuals as to church, conference, and jurisdictional membership; freedom of choice also to conferences and to churches as to the way and manner of their association and membership.

No barriers should be placed in the way of the working out of the free choice of individuals who agree in their choice.[17]

Having seen and heard of other groups within the church who would welcome African American churches, the bishops wanted to make it clear that this should be encouraged.

The bishops of the Central Jurisdiction went on to underscore the significance of the race problem in America, whatever the church might choose to do.

Whether or not the Central Jurisdiction is continued as such within the church, whether or not jurisdictions will continue as a part of the church, certainly the race problem belongs not alone to the top level, such as the jurisdictional boundaries.[18]

The year 1952 was a time when the jurisdictions, having found a way of working as structures, could turn their attention to the dilemma that was always in the background—the Central Jurisdiction.

NOTES

1. General Conference, 1948, *The Daily Christian Advocate*, April 29, 1948, p. 35.
2. Ibid., p. 64.
3. See John H. Graham, *Black United Methodists: Retrospect and Prospect*, (New York: Vantage Press, 1979), p. 94.
4. *Journal of the Third Central Jurisdictional Conference of The Methodist Church*, vol. 3, p. 125.
5. Ibid., pp. 163-64.
6. Ibid., p. 67.
7. Ibid., p. 68.
8. Ibid., p. 81.
9. Ibid., p. 82.
10. Ibid., p. 114.

11. Ibid., p. 137.
12. General Conference of 1952, *The Daily Christian Advocate*, April 24, 1952, p. 64.
13. Ibid.
14. Ibid.
15. *Journal of the Fourth Session of the Central Jurisdictional Conference of The Methodist Church*, vol. 4, p. 91.
16. Ibid., p. 142.
17. Ibid., pp. 143-44.
18. Ibid., p. 144.

A Look at the
Jurisdictional System

Among those who were against the Central Jurisdiction, two broad groups could be identified. They were (1) those who opposed the jurisdictional system as a way of doing the business of the church, and (2) those who specifically opposed the Central Jurisdiction on the basis of racial segregation. Sometimes it was hard to tell one group from the other; sometimes the groups overlapped; and sometimes the opponent of one began at one point and became the opponent of the other as the debate progressed.

However one might divide the points of view, it became clear very early in the General Conference that the jurisdictional system would become a dominant issue in 1956. The General Conference opened in Minneapolis, Minnesota, on Wednesday, April 25. On Thursday morning, April 26, a resolution was presented by Harold A. Bosley of the Rock River Conference. The resolution had six points. It took into account the Episcopal Address that had recognized the need "of an immediate and thorough review of the philosophy and effectiveness of the Jurisdictional structures of government began seventeen years ago with the unification of the three branches of American Methodism."[1]

The resolution went on to request, in its first major point:

1) That this General Conference constitute a Commission for such study, the same to be elected by the General Conference on nomination by the Council of Bishops, as follows: two bishops, two ministers, and two lay persons from each

Jurisdiction; and in addition, one minister and one lay person for each five hundred thousand church members or major fraction thereof in each Jurisdiction. Vacancies occurring during the quadrennium shall be filled in each instance by the College of Bishops of the Jurisdiction concerned.

The main purpose of this Commission would be (a) to review the philosophy of the Jurisdictional system as an instrument of unity in the church. A second point was (b) to ascertain the effects of the Jurisdictional system on the separate Jurisdictions and on the church as a whole.[2]

No mention is made about the Central Jurisdiction in the resolution. However, it was clear that when a commission began to "ascertain the effects of the Jurisdictional system on the separate Jurisdictions," it would have to treat the Central Jurisdiction as the separate racial jurisdiction that it was.

The presenter of this resolution, Harold Bosley, moved reference of the resolution to the Committee on Conferences.

Immediately after reference was moved, a member of the General Conference, Chester A. Smith of New York, rose to speak against it. He began by saying: "We have come to a critical and most important matter which I think will come before this General Conference at this session; namely, the question of segregation of the 350,000 Negro members of the Methodist Church."[3] Mr. Smith went on to propose "an amendment to the Constitution which, if adopted by the necessary two-thirds of the Annual Conferences, would abolish the Central Jurisdiction, put the Annual Conferences now in the Central Jurisdiction in such remaining jurisdictions under the plan of union as might be mutually agreeable to those Annual Conferences and the remaining Jurisdictions."[4]

The speaker went on to refer to the recent Supreme Court decision on public school education. He concluded: "There is, therefore, only one thing for us to do. We cannot tolerate segregation in the Methodist Church any longer."[5]

There was now no way to avoid specific reference to the Central Jurisdiction. What may have been implicit in the resolution by Harold Bosley was made quite clear and explicit by Chester A. Smith. After some debate, the resolution was referred to the Committee on Conferences. Referral of the report did not get the issue of segregation off the floor. After referral of the Smith resolution, Thurman L. Dodson, a member of the Central Jurisdiction, offered a resolution on segregation. His resolution was also of six points. In point five, Mr. Dodson asked "that this Conference here and now abolish all forms of segregation so far as this General Conference may so do."[6] He also called upon the General Conference to "reaffirm our belief that segregation and discrimination are sinful and contrary to the teachings of Christ."[7] Mr. Dodson moved to refer his resolution to the Committee on Conferences.

Even though the committees of the General Conference had not yet begun their work, it became clear that many members of this General Conference wanted to have a general discussion of segregation and specific discussion of the Central Jurisdiction. A motion by Chester A. Smith was made that the General Conference instruct the Committee on the State of the Church to bring in a constitutional amendment that would abolish the Central Jurisdiction.

During the same day a resolution on segregation in The Methodist Publishing House was presented to the General Conference. A little later, a member of the General Conference presented another resolution to create a commission to study the Jurisdictional system. It was referred to the Committee on Conferences.

When the Committee on the State of the Church made its first report, it presented to the General Conference a clear and strong position against segregation: "The teaching of our Lord is that all men are brothers. The Master permits no discrimination because of race, color, or national origin."[8] The report went on to recognize the changing climate in the world.

There is a changing racial climate in our world, largely growing out of the teachings of the Christian church. The conscience of society has been increasingly sensitive regarding racial discrimination and injustice. Methodists unite with people of all lands and all faiths in a determined effort to eliminate these unchristian practices. We look to the ultimate establishment of a truly Christian society.[9]

Having said this much, the report set the stage for even more intense discussions and debate on the Central Jurisdiction as a racial unit in the church. Urged on by many resolutions and petitions, the Committee on the State of the Church of the 1956 General Conference had taken such high ground in its statements on race that no retreat from that position would be possible in the future.

Having made its first report, both the members of the Committee on Conferences and members of the Committee on the State of the Church recognized the pressure of public opinion. On Wednesday, May 2, 1956, *The Daily Christian Advocate* quoted Charles C. Parlin, Chairman of the Committee on the State of the Church, as saying:

The eyes of Methodists are upon this body at this hour. I am told since I came to Minneapolis that the drafting committees of both the Republican and Democratic parties are awaiting to see what this Christian group coming from every section of the land can say on the subject of race.[10]

The dilemma at this point was facing the reluctance to abolish the Central Jurisdiction by many within The Methodist Church and, at the same time, facing a growing public conscience against segregation by many outside the church.

Two Ways Out

On Thursday, May 3, *The Daily Christian Advocate* reported that C. Cooper Bell, of the Committee on Conferences, made a statement to the General Conference that he called a miracle. He presented Leonard Slutz who, reporting for the Committee, presented two constitutional amendments. The first constitutional amendment is so central to any study of the Central Jurisdiction that it will be quoted in full.

The Constitution of the Methodist Church shall be amended by adding a new Article to be known as Article V of Division Two, Section VIII and to read as follows:
a) A local church may transfer from one Annual Conference to another in which it is geographically located upon approval by a ⅔ vote by those present and voting in each of the following:
1. The Quarterly Conference of the local church.
2. A Church Conference of the local church.
3. Each of the two Annual Conferences involved.
The vote shall be certified by the Secretaries of the specified Conference to the Bishops having supervision of the Annual Conferences involved, and upon their announcement of the required majorities the transfer shall be immediately effective.
b) An Annual Conference may transfer from one Jurisdiction to another upon approval by:
1. The Annual Conference desiring transfer, by a ⅔ majority of those present and voting. The Secretary of the Conference shall certify the vote to the College of Bishops of the Jurisdiction of which the Conference has been a part.
2. The remainder of the Jurisdiction from which transfer is to be made, by a ⅔ majority of the total . . ."

Mr. Slutz went on to explain that this meant "⅔ majority of the total Annual Conference members present and voting."

The vote shall be taken in the other Annual Conferences of the Jurisdiction and certified by their Secretaries to the College of Bishops which shall determine whether ⅔ of the total vote is favorable.

3. The Jurisdiction to which transfer is to be made, by a ⅔ majority of the total of those present and voting. The vote shall be taken in the various Annual Conferences of the Jurisdiction and certified by their Secretaries to the College of Bishops which shall determine whether ⅔ of the total vote in the Jurisdiction is favorable.

Upon announcement by the two College of Bishops of the required majorities the transfer shall immediately be effective. Transfers under provisions of this Article shall not be governed or restricted by other provisions of this Constitution relating to change of boundaries of conferences.[11]

At this point, Leonard Slutz made an amendment to the report, as follows:

Whenever 25 percent of the membership of the Central Jurisdiction have been transferred by this process to another Jurisdiction or Jurisdictions, the bishop of the Area from which the largest number have been transferred shall be transferred to the Jurisdiction which has received the largest number by such transfer, and the representation of the Central Jurisdiction on the boards and agencies of the church shall thereafter be proportionately reduced.[12]

After some discussion with the presiding officer of the General Conference, Leonard Slutz presented another amendment for the action of the General Conference. He wanted to add a new paragraph to the one describing the Jurisdictions.

> *Abolition of the Central Jurisdiction:* The Central Jurisdiction shall be abolished when all of the Annual Conferences now comprising it have transferred to and have been accepted by another Jurisdiction or Jurisdictions in accordance with the voluntary procedure of Article V of this section.[13]

After some discussion, it was moved that the report be deferred. One of the speakers in support of deferment was Thelma Stevens. Her objection was that there had not been adequate study. She said: "When we begin the process of emasculating the Central Jurisdiction, it will go over a long period of years and will be an unfair placing of that Jurisdiction in terms of its total leadership."[14] She went on to make a second point: "The second thing is I think we recognize this amendment as another delaying tactic to keep this General Conference from making its clear-cut statement on the fact that The Methodist Church has arrived at that period in its history."[15]

In the discussion were two members of the Central Jurisdiction. One of them, Thurman L. Dodson, who presented an earlier resolution on integration, said:

> Mr. Chairman, I want to speak in favor of this motion that is now before us, on the adoption of these constitutional amendments. I want to say that we appreciate all of the shortcoming of this resolution, as far as it goes. We are not being fooled at all by it. We realize that this amendment does not abolish segregation in The Methodist Church. But it does move in a direction toward which this great church of ours ought to move.[16]

Dodson felt that these constitutional amendments helped to eradicate a rigidity on the Central Jurisdiction that was presently in the Constitution. It would, he felt, "provide a fluidity which ought to be in a great church which is as complex and heterogeneous as this church is."[17]

Chester A. Smith offered a substitute for the constitutional amendments proposed by Leonard Slutz. He moved that

> we submit to the Annual Conferences of the church an amendment to the Constitution which if adopted would abolish the Central Jurisdiction and place the Annual Conferences in that Jurisdiction in such remaining Jurisdictions as will be agreeable to those Jurisdictions and to the Annual Conferences of the former Central Jurisdiction.[18]

This substitute was lost.

On Tuesday, May 3, 1956, the General Conference adopted two provisions amending the Constitution and providing a voluntary way by which the Central Jurisdiction could, in time, be abolished.

Another important action of the 1956 General Conference was to adopt a report calling for a Commission to Study and Recommend Action Concerning the Jurisdictional System. The report of the Committee on Conferences was similar to the resolution offered by Harold A. Bosley on Thursday morning, April 26, 1956. The later report contained at least one provision that was not in the Bosley resolution. It was: "3. To develop courses of action directed towards greater interracial brotherhood and the spirit of Christian love."[19]

The resolution, as adopted by the General Conference was a response to many appeals from the wider church. Its preamble began by saying:

> In response to the numerous memorials and resolutions before this General Conference requesting a study of the structure of the Jurisdictional System, and to implement the recommendations contained in the Episcopal Addresses of 1952 and 1956; . . . We hereby recommend that the General Conference of 1956 create a "Commission to Study and Recommend Action Concerning the Jurisdictional System."[20]

In this way, the immediate dilemma was resolved or at least deferred.

Actions of the Central Jurisdiction

The fifth session of the Central Jurisdictional Conference opened on Wednesday, June 13, 1956, at Dillard University in New Orleans. It was a relatively quiet session from the standpoint of actions taken. There were two outstanding events: the election of a bishop and the report of the Commission to Study the Central Jurisdiction first organized in 1948.

On the first day of the Jurisdictional Conference, Wednesday, June 13, James P. Brawley moved that an order of the day be set on Friday morning, June 15. The order was set for that time.

As Brawley was reading his report, he was interrupted to hear the report on the first episcopal ballot. When the visiting bishop from the North Central Jurisdiction was presented, he expressed appreciation for the report of the Commission to Study the Central Jurisdiction. The Jurisdictional Conference continued to ballot for a General Superintendent in between the Committee reports and fraternal greetings. On ballot number 9, Prince A. Taylor, Jr. was elected as the ninth bishop of the Central Jurisdiction. He was assigned to Liberia.

Report of the Commission to Study the Central Jurisdiction

The report of the Commission to Study the Central Jurisdiction was so thorough that it was highly commended by the Jurisdictional Conference. On Saturday, June 16, 1956, a layman from the Lexington Conference, Joseph T. Johnson, asked for the privilege of the floor. He moved that the "Fifth Central Jurisdictional Conference express their sincere gratitude to Dr. James P. Brawley and the members of the Commission to Study the Central Jurisdiction for the excellent work done in the study, preparation, and presentation of the fine report brought to the conference."[21] The motion was seconded and carried.

The Commission's report considered five factors as necessary to an understanding of the perplexing problems of the Central Jurisdiction. These were:

1) Its Geographical Expanse and Overlapping
2) Unrelatedness to Other Jurisdictions
3) Advantages and Disadvantages
4) Types of Modification Already Effected
5) Pending Modifications

Under geographical expanse the report noted that the St. Louis Area of the Central Jurisdiction touched eighteen states. It extended from Butte, Montana, on the north to Muskogee, Oklahoma on the south, and from Youngstown, Ohio, on the east to Denver on the west. The report went on to point out that the Baltimore Area reached nine states, the Atlantic Coast covered four states, and the New Orleans Area covered three states.

The report summarized the geographical problem by pointing out that "geographically, the four areas of the Central Jurisdiction overlap or reach into the territory of all the effective bishops resident in the United States except in Boston, Los Angeles, Portland, and San Francisco Areas."[22]

With this kind of overlap, there would be a duplication of functions. The Commission sent a questionnaire to all the bishops resident in the United States. In their reply several bishops pointed to the fact that the church suffers because of this duplication "in that many territories the white churches are not at all conscious of the presence of the Negro churches of the Methodist church within the town or community and there is little or no cooperation or recognition of the need of such on the part of the people of the two races within the same community."[23]

The report made several recommendations. Among them were these:

> Ask for interracial conferences without segregation.
>
> Ask the General Church to face frankly the responsibility of removing legal barriers that affect the whole Church and prohibit free communication and the establishment of interracial churches where this is desired and can be worked out with mutual satisfaction.[24]

Concern was expressed that Methodists would too easily forget the statements on race that were being made by such organizations as the World Council of Churches and groups within The Methodist Church. It was reported that the Central Pennsylvania Conference approved the transfer of the only Negro church within its bounds into the Conference.

The report outlined seven ways of dealing with the Central Jurisdiction in 1956. These were:

1. *Attrition*
   There were those who think of solving the problem of the Central Jurisdiction by transferring church by church into those regional jurisdictions that would accept this procedure.

2. *Dispersal*
   Creating five Central Jurisdictional Areas, with Liberia being one of them. These would then be dispersed throughout the general work of the church.

3. *Semantic*
   This method calls for a constitutional change that would strike the words "Negro" and "colored" from any reference to boundaries. Otherwise the present character of the Jurisdictions would remain unchanged.

4. *Dissolution*

The church should remove segregation from its constitutional structure and administrative practices. It would, in short, adopt the proposal made by Thurman Dodson in the 1956 General Conference.

5. *Functional*

"The main issue is the creation of a positive Christian fellowship which is thoroughly integrated, not only by Jurisdictional or Conference rearrangement, but by local creative fellowships."[25]

6. *Absorption*

The Central Jurisdiction absorbed into other jurisdictions with a gentleman's agreement that as long as there are dominant Negro areas, churches, and conferences, the Central Jurisdiction will have with it Negro district superintendents and bishops.

7. *Static*

The present jurisdictional system would be preserved as it is.

During the quadrennium, articles were written, speeches were made, and proposals were set forth representing one or the other of these general points of view.

The report presented a clear outline of the advantages and disadvantages of the Central Jurisdiction. Among the eleven advantages were these:

1. It provides equal status and privileges of action.

2. It guarantees representation in cases where numbers in Negro membership would not entitle that representation.

3. It offers a framework within which to operate on an unequal representation basis to work toward desegregation and integration in The Methodist Church.

Among the disadvantages of the Central Jurisdiction were these:

1. The Central Jurisdiction is the medium used to segregate Negro Churches and membership of The Methodist Church, and to close the channels of free communication between Negro and white churches.

2. The legal arrangements perpetuate segregation in the church.

3. Further, the Central Jurisdiction arrangement prohibits free fellowship and free admission of Negro churches into the white conferences where there is a mutual desire for such fellowship and membership. If the law does not prohibit this free fellowship and admission of Negro churches to white conferences in other jurisdictions, the arrangements by which this might be done are so cumbersome and time-consuming that it is tantamount to being prohibitive.[26]

The Commission to Study the Central Jurisdiction also sent out a questionnaire to a cross-section of ministerial and lay leadership of the Central Jurisdiction. Seventy-six percent of those who responded favored the abolition of the Central Jurisdiction in its present form.

When the respondents to the questionnaire were asked to list the favorable qualities of the Central Jurisdiction, their answers tended to fall into four categories. Two of these were:

1. Opportunity for the expression of a Negro leadership within the Church structure,
2. The development of consensus within the Negro group and pride in its own achievement.[27]

In its summary and conclusions, the Commission to Study the Central Jurisdiction began by saying that "segregation in The Methodist Church is legalized through the Constitution, the basic Plan of Union."[28]

It went on to say:

> There is one thing on which all Negroes could and should be together and that is the fact that we oppose segregation in the Church, in the community, and in our national life; therefore every conference should request the General Conference to oppose strongly and unrelentingly all forms of racial segregation and to authorize a program that would begin immediately to remove segregation on all levels of relationship in the Methodist Church.[29]

In its final summary statement, the Commission joined the many voices of the 1956 General Conference asking for an interjurisdictional commission to study segregation in the church. It called upon the Central Jurisdictional Conference to ask the General Conference for an interjurisdictional commission for the next quadrennium charged with the specific functions of studying segregation in the church and the formulation of plans and programs to eliminate segregation.[30]

The force of this statement left little doubt as to the majority feelings of the leaders of the Central Jurisdiction. After sixteen years of working as a Jurisdiction, and admitting the benefit of a close fellowship, these leaders, influenced heavily by the events going on around them, called for nothing less than the total elimination of segregation from the national and ecclesiastical life of the United States.

NOTES

1. General Conference, 1956, *The Daily Christian Advocate*, April 26, 1956, p. 85.
2. Ibid.

3. Ibid., p. 86.
4. Ibid.
5. Ibid.
6. Ibid., p. 88.
7. Ibid.
8. Ibid., p. 198.
9. Ibid.
10. Ibid., p. 276.
11. General Conference, 1956, *The Daily Christian Advocate*, May 3, 1956, pp. 358-59.
12. Ibid.
13. Ibid.
14. Ibid., p. 362.
15. Ibid.
16. Ibid.
17. Ibid., p. 363.
18. Ibid., p. 364.
19. Ibid., p. 245.
20. Ibid., p. 244.
21. *Journal of the Fifth Session of the Central Jurisdictional Conference*, 1956, p. 112.
22. Ibid., pp. 170, 171.
23. Ibid., p. 171.
24. Ibid., p. 200.
25. Ibid., p. 189.
26. Ibid., pp. 192, 193.
27. Ibid., p. 195.
28. Ibid., p. 199.
29. Ibid., p. 200.
30. Ibid.

Amendment IX and the Central Jurisdiction Study Committee

T he actions of the 1956 General Conference, ordering a study of the Jurisdictional System, should be seen in the light of action already taken in 1952. Facing mounting pressure to abolish the Central Jurisdiction, the General Conference of 1952 provided a way whereby this might be done.

The provision was not in the Constitution. It appeared as paragraph 538 under "Jurisdictional Boundaries."

> Any local church shall be transferred from the jurisdiction of which it is a part to another jurisdiction in which it is located geographically upon completion of all the following actions, regardless of the order in which taken: (a) approval by the membership of the quarterly Conference of said church; (b) approval by both the Annual Conference of which the church has been a part and the Annual Conference to which transfer is desired; (c) approval by a majority of the Annual Conferences and also by the Jurisdictional Conference of both the jurisdiction of which the church has been a part and the jurisdiction to which transfer is desired; and (d) approval by the General Conference in the form of an enabling act. Such transfer shall be effected when all of the required actions have been certified to the Council of Bishops by the secretaries of all the Conferences involved, whereupon the Council of Bishops shall issue a declaration that the transfer has been duly effected.[1]

This provision was adopted following five decisions by the Judicial Council.

99

While no mention is made of the Central Jurisdiction in this paragraph, it was clearly intended to allow for transfers of churches from the only nongeographical jurisdiction to others with geographical boundaries.

When, therefore, Amendment IX to the Constitution was adopted in 1956, it was not without some precedent. In fact, there is some similarity between the provision of 1952 and that of 1956. A part of this story appears in the Constitution of 1956, as follows:

> See Judicial Council Decision 128. The General Conference of 1956 proposed and referred to the members of the several Annual Conferences as Amendment IX the following: Add at the end of Article I of Division Two, Section VIII (¶ 26): *Abolition of the Central Jurisdiction.*—The Central Jurisdiction shall be abolished when all of the Annual Conferences now comprising it have been transferred to other jurisdictions in accordance with the voluntary procedure of Article V of this section. Each remaining bishop of the Central Jurisdiction shall thereupon be transferred to the jurisdiction to which the majority of the membership of his area have been transferred, and the Central Jurisdiction shall then be dissolved.

Then a new article was added on the local church:

> Article V.—1. A local church may be transferred from one Annual Conference to another in which it is geographically located upon approval by a two-thirds vote of those present and voting in each of the following:
>   a) The Quarterly Conference of the local church.
>   b) A Church Conference of the local church.
>   c) Each of the two Annual Conferences involved.
> The vote shall be certified by the secretaries of the specified conferences to the bishops having supervision of the Annual Conferences involved, and upon their announcement of the required majorities the transfer shall be immediately effective.

2. An Annual Conference may be transferred from one jurisdiction to another upon approval by:

a) The Annual Conference desiring transfer, by a two-thirds majority of those present and voting. The secretary of the conference shall certify the vote to the College of Bishops of the jurisdiction of which the conference has been a part.[2]

It had been seventeen years since the Central Jurisdiction came into existence through an act of the Constitution. Now, another act of the Constitution provided a way out of the dilemma presented by the existence of the Central Jurisdiction.

The Bishops Speak

Writing in a section entitled "The Jurisdictional System and Racial Brotherhood," the bishops expressed deep concern both for the jurisdictional system and racial brotherhood. They pointed to previous statements and actions of the General Conferences of 1952 and 1956. Also, they repeated the statement made in these General Conferences: "To discriminate against a person solely on the basis of his race is both unfair and unchristian," and "There must be no place in The Methodist Church for racial discrimination or enforced segregation."[3]

The episcopal address went on to admit the failure of the church in all sections: "Our failure thus far to achieve the aims of Christian brotherhood is a fault that must be shared by every section of the Church."[4] There was also a strong statement (against racial segregation) "The pattern of the relations between the races, based upon any theory of superiority-inferiority, has been shattered beyond reassertion in secular life and in the Church."[5]

After having been passed by the required aggregate number of those voting in the Annual Conferences,

Amendment IX to the Constitution of The Methodist Church appeared in this form:

Abolition of the Central Jurisdiction.
The Central Jurisdiction shall be abolished when all of the Annual Conferences now comprising it have been transferred to other jurisdictions in accordance with the voluntary procedure of Article V of this section. Each remaining bishop of the Central Jurisdiction shall thereupon be transferred to the jurisdiction to which the majority of the membership of his area have been transferred, and the Central Jurisdiction shall then be dissolved.
Article V
1. A local church may be transferred from one Annual Conference to another in which it is geographically located upon approval by a two-thirds vote of those present and voting in each of the following:
a) The Quarterly Conference of the local church.
b) A Church Conference of the local church.
c) Each of the two Annual Conferences involved.
The vote shall be certified by the secretaries of the specified conferences to the bishops having supervision of the Annual Conferences involved, and upon their announcement of the required majorities the transfer shall immediately be effective.
2. An Annual Conference may be transferred from one jurisdiction to another upon approval by:

a) The Annual Conference desiring transfer, by a two-thirds majority of those present and voting. The secretary of the conference shall certify the vote to the College of Bishops of the jurisdiction of which the conference has been a part.
b) The remainder of the jurisdiction from which the transfer is to be made, by a two-thirds majority of the total of those present and voting. The vote shall be taken in the other Annual Conferences of the jurisdiction and certified by their secretaries to the College of Bishops, which shall determine

whether two-thirds of the total vote in the jurisdiction is favorable.

c) The jurisdiction to which transfer is to be made, by a two-thirds majority of the total of Annual Conference members present and voting. The vote shall be taken in the various Annual Conferences of the jurisdiction and certified by their secretaries to the College of Bishops, which shall determine whether two-thirds of the total vote in the jurisdiction is favorable.

Upon announcement by the two Colleges of Bishops of the required majorities the transfer shall immediately be effective.

3. The vote on approval of transfer under either Section 1 or Section 2 [of this article] shall be taken by each Annual Conference at its first session after the matter is submitted to it.

4. Transfers under the provisions of this article shall not be governed or restricted by other provisions of this Constitution relating to changes of boundaries of conferences.

5. Whenever twenty-five percent of the local-church membership of the Central Jurisdiction have been transferred by this process to another jurisdiction or jurisdictions, the bishop of the area from which the largest number have been transferred shall be transferred to the jurisdiction which has received the largest number by such transfer, and the representation of the Central Jurisdiction on the boards, agencies, and episcopacy of the church shall thereafter be proportionately reduced.[6]

The bishops urged the General Conference to give careful attention to the report of the Commission to Study and Recommend Action Concerning the Jurisdictional System.

It is not without significance that the writer of the Episcopal Address, Bishop William C. Martin, a bishop of the South Central Jurisdiction, was himself a Southerner. The Central Jurisdiction was not mentioned by name in the section on the Jurisdictional System, but it was clear that racial brotherhood had specific meaning for the bishops of The Methodist Church.

The Report of the Commission

The Commission authorized by the 1956 General Conference had a wider task than consideration of the Central Jurisdiction. It was to consider the Jurisdictional System as a structure for doing the business of the church. One section of the report did deal with "The Jurisdiction Based on Race." The Commission's report in this section was highly criticized by many leaders of the Central Jurisdiction. One of the reasons for this criticism was that the Commission offered no plan for the inclusion of local churches and annual conferences other than the provision of Amendment IX. In one place the Commission's report said:

> The abolition at this time of the Central Jurisdiction would impose hardships on its constituent Annual Conferences. If the Jurisdiction were abolished, these Annual Conferences would be immediately forced to one of two alternatives: 1) remain separate and not a part of any jurisdiction or 2) join any jurisdiction which has extended or may extend an invitation.[7]

Even though the Commission estimated that less than 1 percent of the Central Jurisdiction local churches had been transferred under the provisions of Amendment IX, it recommended "that the General Conference of 1960 undertake no basic change in the Central Jurisdiction."[8]

The leaders of the Central Jurisdiction felt that a failure to put forth a specific plan of inclusion was a very serious one. They could see several outcomes, none of them very satisfactory.

1) If enough large and successful local churches went to other annual conferences by way of Amendment IX, it would

eventually leave small and struggling local churches in the Central Jurisdiction.

2) If enough annual conferences went to other jurisdictions, by way of Amendment IX, it would likewise leave a few small annual conferences with little ability to negotiate.

There seemed to be little reason to expect any more than another 1 percent of transfer by way of Amendment IX in the next quadrennium.

What was needed was a carefully devised plan which would allow annual conferences to transfer, on schedule, without having to go through so many steps. There was a need for an agreement with jurisdictions that the annual conferences within their geographic area would be included according to a mutually agreed upon plan.

The Commission's report did make several recommendations to increase racial understanding, but it was this negative recommendation—no change in the Central Jurisdiction—that stayed in the minds of leaders of the Central Jurisdiction.

When the Commission's report was presented to the General Conference of 1960, there was a very long and extended debate. Much of the debate was on other issues than the Central Jurisdiction, but adequate attention was given the matters of race.

At one point, an African American delegate asked for a time line by which the Central Jurisdiction would be included in the geographic jurisdictions. This was defeated.

Perhaps the sharpest recommendation came to the floor from Edwin L. Jones of North Carolina. He proposed "that we frame a constitutional amendment to abolish the Central Jurisdiction and to divide it between the Northeastern and North Central Jurisdictions."[9] This proposal initiated a great deal of debate but did not pass.

In spite of strong opposition to the negative recommendation of Amendment IX, one leading African American leader spoke for it. On Monday, May 3, 1960, James P. Brawley took the floor and said: "The due constitutional process is inherent in Amendment IX and I think that Amendment IX is the process by, the Constitutional process by which we ought to proceed."[10]

The Constitutional process of Amendment IX had the value of providing a way out of a dilemma. And even though it had the faults of being too complex and also too hazardous for the church seeking transfer, it was, after all, an improvement over no way out.

The debate over the Central Jurisdiction and other points about the jurisdictional system continued for parts of four days and nights. Finally, the debate ended with most of the Commission's report being adopted.

The Central Jurisdiction Speaks

The sixth session of the Central Jurisdictional Conference opened in Cory Methodist Church in Cleveland, Ohio, on July 13, 1960. On the second day of the conference, James P. Brawley presented a resolution with two important points:

Resolved.
1. That the Central Jurisdiction look with favor upon the action taken by the West Wisconsin Annual Conference and encourage the transfer of that Conference into the Central Jurisdiction.
2. That the invitation of the North Central Jurisdiction to transfer the St. Louis Area or conferences within that geographical location into that Jurisdiction be accepted, tentatively, pending the working out of satisfactory details, working toward the end of making transfers by the end of this quadrennium, 1960–1964.[11]

For the first time a geographical jurisdiction made important steps toward the inclusion of the Central

Jurisdiction. One of its Annual Conferences would join the Central Jurisdiction and the conferences of the St. Louis Area could and would become a part of the North Central Jurisdiction. It was this kind of action that the leaders of the Central Jurisdiction considered to be highly important.

The Sixth Session of the Central Jurisdictional Conference elected three bishops: Charles F. Golden, Noah W. Moore, and Marquis L. Harris.

The episcopal address of the bishops of the Central Jurisdiction spoke to the broader issues of The Methodist Church, with very little emphasis upon the Central Jurisdiction. At one point the address spoke to the broader concerns of African Americans in the Church.

> Our struggles are for the right to move freely and to share in the total experience of our culture. We understand what is involved. We do not wish to take over churches; we do not wish to visit in churches unless invited; but, if invited, we feel that there should be no reprisals; we want to be men in our country and in our Church.[12]

The bishops also endorsed the report of the Commission to Study the Jurisdictional System. They said:

> The General Conference adopted the report of the Special Study Commission—continuing the Jurisdictional system but setting up a Commission on Inter-Jurisdictional Relations. We should take every advantage of this Special Commission and its findings to develop a strategy for our own approach to the problem.[13]

Amendment IX, then, with obvious faults and complexities, would be used to the limit of its effectiveness.

The Committee of Five

The sixth session of the Central Jurisdictional Conference authorized a Committee of five persons, one from each

Episcopal Area, to do a study of the Central Jurisdiction. The authorization was clearly aimed at making the Central Jurisdiction a part of any plan for its elimination and inclusion. The Committee was to work with any agencies, commissions, or persons who had as their goal the inclusion of the Central Jurisdiction. It was resolved:

> That a jurisdictional committee be created for the quadrennium 1960–64 consisting of five members, one from each area, to work in conjunction with the jurisdictional Committee on Christian Social Concerns and the representatives of the Commission on Interjurisdictional Relations and to study the broader aspects of problems and adjustments, as follows:[14]

Five areas of study were then outlined.

The key to the Committee's work was this injunction: "That in the first year of the quadrennium the Committee shall give special attention to the methods and procedures by which the Central Jurisdiction may be dissolved."[15]

On November 29, 1960, I received a letter from Bishop Edgar A. Love informing me that I had been appointed to the Committee and asking me to call the Committee at my nearest convenience.

The Committee was comprised of: Richard C. Erwin of the Baltimore Area, a layman and lawyer; the Reverend John H. Graham of the Nashville-Birmingham Area, staff member, General Board of Missions; William Astor Kirk of the New Orleans Area, a layman and staff member of the General Board of Christian Social Concerns; the Reverend John J. Hicks, Pastor, Union Memorial Church, St Louis Area; the Reverend James S. Thomas, staff member, General Board of Education, Atlantic Coast Area.

Within a few weeks the Committee met to consider its task and to get under way with its work. Understanding its mission to be both working with other committees or commissions and developing its own plans, the Central Jurisdiction Study

Committee began a series of meetings and consultations in various sections of the Jurisdiction. The Committee met with the African American members of the Commission on Interjurisdictional Relations, with the College of Bishops of the Central Jurisdiction, and with many persons and groups who wanted to know the point of view of the Central Jurisdiction's leaders.

The Cincinnati Exploratory Meeting

As might be expected, there were many kinds of attitudes and beliefs in the Central Jurisdiction. Some expressed publicly a desire for the elimination of the Central Jurisdiction, but felt privately that the Central Jurisdiction might be a good thing, at least for awhile. Others, in local churches, wanted to transfer out of the jurisdiction as soon as possible, using the provisions of Amendment IX. Still others were debating the issue with no firm views on either side.

Sensing these varied points of view, the College of Bishops of the Central Jurisdiction called the Cincinnati Exploratory Meeting for March 26–28, 1962. The purpose of the meeting was to explore the different points of view and to seek a common mind on the major objections of Central Jurisdiction leadership.

Following the meeting in Cincinnati, a brochure was published by Bishop Charles F. Golden, General Chairman of the Conference, and James S. Thomas. The last paragraph of that statement is a succinct summary of the Conference:

> The spirit of the Study Conference has been variously interpreted. But those who worked closest with the sessions have remarked upon its seriousness and its sensitiveness to responsibility. This report is presented in the hope that all future work on the Central Jurisdiction may continue under the guidance of God and in a similar spirit.[16]

The Cincinnati Conference did its work in thirteen group meetings. Many points of view were presented and debated. A committee coordinated the data. Before the meeting was over, an unusual consensus emerged on major purposes and goals. The purpose of the Conference was achieved to a very large degree.

Writings of the Committee to Study the Central Jurisdiction

The Committee to Study the Central Jurisdiction sensed both confusion and hesitance among Central Jurisdiction local churches to use Amendment IX as a vehicle for transfer. The same was true of annual conferences. There were varied reasons for this hesitancy. What if a local church desiring to transfer met with thinly veiled rebuff or reluctance from the other side? What if one of the several groups that had to agree to transfer demurred for what it considered to be good and sufficient reasons? Another way had to be found to facilitate transfer of local churches and annual conferences.

The Committee to Study the Central Jurisdiction tried to fill the vacuum by providing several publications that were widely distributed to leaders and members of the jurisdiction. These were:

1. A Study Document on Realignment of the Central Jurisdiction
2. The Creative Pursuit of an Inclusive Church
3. Plan of Action for the Elimination of the Central Jurisdiction
4. Bridges to Racial Equality in The Methodist Church

The Study Document was a follow-up to the Cincinnati Exploratory meeting. It set forth a realignment of the annual conferences of the Central Jurisdiction.

The Cincinnati Study Conference proposed that the 1964 Central Jurisdictional Conference realign the boundaries of its annual conferences "so that each Conference will be located within the boundary of not more than one regional jurisdiction." It recommended that the Central Jurisdiction Study Committee (Committee of Five), in consultation with the College of Bishops and selected church leaders, develop a realignment plan "for presentation to the 1964 Jurisdictional Conference."[17]

This is in fact what the Committee to Study the Central Jurisdiction did. It presented for study a document complete with maps, membership of annual conferences, and number of local churches.

Even though the Commission to Study and Recommend Action Concerning the Jurisdictional System had called for a realignment of Central Jurisdiction Annual Conferences, it failed to understand either the Cincinnati Study Conference or the Study Document. On June 21, 1962, Charles C. Parlin, the chairman of the new Commission on Interjurisdictional Relations, wrote a letter to W. Astor Kirk and James S. Thomas expressing great hope in Amendment IX. Then, referring to the report of the earlier Commission, he went on to say:

> The Report of the Commission was well received by the church—I could almost say joyfully—and Annual Conferences went into action.
>
> Then came unilateral action by the Central Jurisdiction, the Committee of Five calling an unofficial, non-disciplinary meeting which recommended action against the Commission's report and urged a further period of study to be followed by realigning of boundaries.[18]

It became clear that the Cincinnati meeting, which was intended to reach some consensus in a jurisdiction that extended over eighteen states, was not understood for what it was.

The CSCJ document, Creative Pursuit of an Inclusive Church, was a series of petitions prepared by the Committee of Five for presentation to the 1964 General Conference. Its purpose was to provide a way by which the high ideals of The Methodist Church could be expressed in its *Book of Discipline*.

In memorial number 3, the Committee to Study the Central Jurisdiction proposed that:

. . . the Discipline be amended by adding to Part IV [the Conferences], Chapter VIII [the Annual Conference], a new paragraph, ¶ 680, to read as follows:

¶ 680. 1. With respect to the procedures under the Constitutional provisions of Division Two, Article V, Section VII (Amendment IX) for the transfer of a local church from one Annual Conference to another and for the transfer of an Annual Conference from one jurisdiction to another, the following rules shall prevail.

2. Whenever a local church votes to transfer from one Annual Conference to another, the votes required by the two Annual Conferences involved shall be effective regardless of the order in which they are taken.

3. Whenever an Annual Conference votes to transfer from one jurisdiction to another, the votes required by the other Annual Conferences of the two jurisdictions involved shall be effective regardless of the order in which they are taken.[19]

This document aimed at placing clear statements of policies and expected practices in the *Book of Discipline*, or amending what was already there.

The Plan of Action for the Elimination of the Central Jurisdiction was a compilation of actions taken by the 1964 General Conference.

The document, Bridges to Racial Equality in The

Methodist Church, was the report of the Central Jurisdiction Study Committee to the Central Jurisdictional Conference of 1964. It will be further discussed in the next chapter.

By the publication and distribution to bishops, district superintendents, and pastors of the Central Jurisdiction of these documents, the people of a wide and diverse jurisdiction became knowledgable about the basic issues of the Central Jurisdiction. What Amendment IX sought to do by general permission, the Central Jurisdiction sought to do by clearly outlined procedures and policies.

It was not so much that Amendment IX was a poor procedure, as that it lacked the bridges by which annual conferences could act in some understandable order and sequence. These bridges needed to be built from both sides and this is what the Central Jurisdiction Study Committee sought to do.

NOTES

1. *Discipline of the Methodist Church*, 1952, par. 538, p. 147.
2. *Discipline of the Methodist Church*, 1956, The Constitution, par. 26, article 1, p. 19.
3. General Conference 1960, *The Daily Christian Advocate*, April 28, 1960, p. 42.
4. Ibid.
5. Ibid.
6. *Discipline of the Methodist Church*, par. 26, pp. 19-20.
7. Report to the 1960 General Conference of the Methodist Church by the Commission to Study and Recommend Action Concerning the Jurisdictional System, p. 10.
8. Ibid., p. 12.
9. General Conference 1960, *The Daily Christian Advocate*, May 2, 1960, p. 180.
10. Ibid., p. 224.
11. *Journal of the Central Jurisdictional Conference*, 1960, p. 81.
12. *Journal of the Sixth Session of the Central Jurisdictional Conference of the Methodist Church*, 1960, p. 138.
13. Ibid.
14. Ibid., p. 72.
15. Ibid.
16. Charles F. Golden and James S. Thomas, *Central Jurisdiction Speaks*, brochure on the Cincinnati Conference, 1962.

17. Study Document on Realignment of the Central Jurisdiction, The Committee of Five, p. 1.
18. Letter from Charles C. Pavlin to James S. Thomas and W. Astor Kirk, June 21, 1962.
19. Creative Pursuit of an Inclusive Church, Memorials to the General Conference, February, 1964, p. 7.

C H A P T E R *8*

A Year of
Decision and Action

From the beginning it became clear that the 1964 General Conference would do something significant about the Central Jurisdiction. In their Episcopal Address, the bishops spoke in unequivocal terms.

> We are dedicated to the proposition that all men are created equal, all men are brothers, and all men are of eternal worth in the eyes of God. Prejudice against any person because of color or social status is a sin.

And even more pointedly:

> We believe that this General Conference should insist upon the removal from its structure any mark of racial segregation and we should do it without wasting time.
> This will cost some Negro Methodists some of their minority rights. It will cost some white Methodists the pain of rooting out deep-seated and long-held convictions concerning race relations. But God Almighty is moving toward a world of interracial brotherhood so speedily and so irresistibly, that to hesitate is to fight against God and be crushed.[1]

This was, by far, the strongest statement on structural segregation ever made by the Council of Bishops.

The Report of the Committee
on Interjurisdictional Relations

As was true of the report of the Commission to Study the Jurisdictional System, the report of the Commission on

Interjurisdictional Relations was made in the early days of the General Conference. Robert A. Raines (an outstanding young pastor) informed me that his sermon would emphasize the need to do away with the structural segregation represented by the Central Jurisdiction. The air was full of determination to do something that was definitive and meaningful.

In his sermon, Raines declared that Methodism's integrity was at stake in the racial decision that must be made at this General Conference. He said that "the nation needs our witness now. Four years from now will be too late. Four years from now no one will listen to us."[2]

Three of the African American members of the Commission on Interjurisdictional Relations presented several amendments to the report. After explaining that there were differences of opinion within the Commission and that the right to express these differences had been safeguarded, John T. King explained:

> Dr. James P. Brawley, Bishop Charles F. Golden and I [King] took advantage of this provision and presented in printed form several amendments to the original report. We are pleased that the Executive Committee adopted some of them. They are included in the amendment to the original report and were in the documents placed on your tables yesterday morning.[3]

Mr. King went on to say:

> To wear my alternate or companion hat, we of the Central Jurisdiction obviously wished to see it eliminated as soon as possible, but be it remembered that we did not create it ourselves. We cannot accept a proposal simply calling for us to abolish the Central Jurisdiction. These proposals are not sufficient in themselves. . . . First we must have a plan so that we can see, or at least anticipate, where we are going to land. . . .[4]

A specific plan for the transfer of annual conferences was lacking in the Commission's report.

General Conference Debate

Once started, the debate on the report of the Commission on Interjurisdictional Relations became long and intense. It varied from Chester Smith's proposal to abolish all jurisdictions (which would of course abolish the Central Jurisdiction) to long discussions on the low pension rates for retired pastors in the Central Jurisdiction.

Several attempts to lay certain sections of the report on the table failed. Instead, the time for debate was often extended. It became clear that this General Conference wanted to debate the report to its end. It also became clear that the debate assumed that the Central Jurisdiction would soon be abolished. The mood was not so much on the "whether" of abolition but on "when."

One member of the General Conference, Allen Mays, spoke the mind of a number of African American delegates when he referred to the lack of a specific plan in the Commission's report. He said:

I believe we must do everything in our power to keep from reverting to a pattern that prevailed in the Methodist Episcopal Church prior to 1939, and without the direction which this proposed amendment would give to the Methodist Church, we could eventually still end up in four years, eight, or even twenty-five years with racially segregated Annual Conferences, in regional jurisdictions as a consequence of the dissolution of the Central Jurisdiction.[5]

Following the trend of the inevitability of the dissolution of the Central Jurisdiction, I offered an amendment to the report of the Commission on Interjurisdictional Relations:

To assist and enable the Commission, in the achievement of the foregoing objectives, each jurisdiction shall establish an advisory council consisting of one member from each Annual Conference with approximately an equal number of ministers and laymen, plus two bishops. The Commission shall arrange for each Council to meet at least once a year, either with the Commission or with one or more of the other councils to consider programs related to transfer and mergers and facilitate such transfers where they may be voted or impeded.[6]

The amendment was adopted.

The Report of the Central Jurisdiction Study Committee

It did not come before the General Conference, but the members of the Commission on Interjurisdictional Relations were aware that the Central Jurisdiction Study Committee had developed a plan for the transfer of annual conferences. According to this plan, the Delaware and Lexington Annual Conferences of the Central Jurisdiction would be realigned and transferred into geographic jurisdictions when the respective Jurisdictional Conferences were held in 1964.

The report of the Central Jurisdiction Study Committee ("Committee of Five") was entitled "Bridges to Racial Equality in the Methodist Church." It did not begin with a plan, but rather with "The Faith That Compels Us." There were seven articles of faith, each beginning with "We Believe." The first of these articles was: "We believe that an inclusive Methodist Church is a society of persons whose life and practice are based on the great Christian affirmation of unity and oneness of all believers in Christ."[7]

The report went on to review the mandate given to the Committee by the 1960 Central Jurisdictional Conference. This was followed by a section on the historical background of the Central Jurisdiction Problem: 1939–1960, and a review of studies of the Central Jurisdiction: 1948–1960.

Attention was given first to the work of the Commission on Interjurisdictional Relations. Then followed a detailed review of the working of the Central Jurisdiction Study Committee, popularly known as the Committee of Five.

It was recommended that the Committee of Five not endorse the first report of the Commission on Interjurisdictional Relations. That Commission made four basic recommendations. That, using Amendment IX:

1) The Delaware, North Carolina, and Washington Annual Conferences be transferred to the Northeastern Jurisdiction;
2) The Central West, Lexington and Southwest Annual Conferences to the South Central Jurisdiction;
3) The Louisiana, Texas, and West Texas Annual Conferences to the South Central Jurisdiction;
4) The Central Alabama, East Tennessee, Florida, Georgia, Mississippi, South Carolina, Tennessee, and Upper Mississippi Annual Conferences to the Southeastern Jurisdiction.

After a comprehensive study and analysis of this plan, the Committee of Five declined to endorse it, giving four reasons for its position.

1) The plan involved both a confusing and indefensible overlapping of supervisory responsibilities of regional jurisdictional Conferences.
2) The plan, as proposed by the Commission of Thirty-Six, involved an expedient shift of major responsibility for dealing with fundamental issues of *de facto* inclusiveness from the general church to the regional Jurisdictions. There was no clear indication of any intention on the part of regional jurisdictional groups (Jurisdictional Conferences, Annual Conferences, Cabinets, etc.) to take definite and specific action to eliminate racial segregation and discrimination.

3) The plan would have institutionalized a system of racially segregated annual conferences in regional Jurisdictions, thereby causing The Methodist Church to revert to the pattern which prevailed in the former Methodist Episcopal Church prior to Unification in 1939.
4) The Commission's plan did not deal with the crucial problems of racial segregation in the government, programs, processes and institutions of The Methodist Church.[8]

The only major change in the Second report of the Commission on Interjurisdictional Relations was the acceptance of a need for the annual conferences of the Central Jurisdiction to be realigned.

During all of the quadrennium of 1960–64, the Central Jurisdiction Study Committee was extremely busy. Both before and after the Cincinnati Exploratory Meeting, members of this Committee of Five were producing memoranda, visiting annual conferences of the Central Jurisdiction to interpret the work of the Committee, visiting and speaking to annual conferences and groups in other Jurisdictions, and producing action brochures that were aimed at the elimination of structural segregation in The Methodist Church.

The Committee of Five differed with the Commission of Thirty-Six in several important ways. In doing so, it made clear that its goal went far beyond "abolishing the Central Jurisdiction." In its basic report, the Committee of Five said:

> To recapitulate, the basic goal of our endeavors, at least as the Committee of Five views it, must be a Methodist Church completely free at all levels of church life of distinctions based on race or color. That means that all forms of racial segregation and discrimination must be eliminated.[9]

With this as a basic goal, the Committee of Five began to concentrate on a plan based upon two important points:

(1) the realignment of the wide-ranging annual conferences of the Central Jurisdiction and (2) the transfer of entire annual conferences from the Central Jurisdiction to regional jurisdictions. This would both eliminate the labored plan of transferring local churches and provide a plan by which the annual conference, now transferred, could become merged with regional annual conferences.

The Committee of Five stated, in its report to the Central Jurisdictional Conference that "it is the belief of the Committee of Five that the Central Jurisdiction should give the higher priority to a programmed implementation of the Annual Conference transfer provision of Amendment IX."[10]

Such a belief would have had no meaning unless there had been many serious consultations with official persons and groups in the jurisdictions that would most likely consider transfers of Central Jurisdiction annual conferences into their regional jurisdictions. These were the North Central and North Eastern Jurisdictions. Out of these consultations came two plans of merger, formally and mutually agreed upon, which, when adopted by the Central Jurisdiction, would transfer the realigned Lexington Annual Conference into the North Central Jurisdiction.

When the Central Jurisdictional Conference adopted the report of the Committee of Five, it also adopted the plans for merger. This was the kind of breakthrough that the Central Jurisdiction Study Committee had in mind when it insisted upon a planned schedule for the merger of annual conferences into regional jurisdictions.

This action, which would become effective upon the meeting of the respective Jurisdictional Conferences, was considered a breakthrough by secular writers as well. In his book *Dark Ghetto*, Kenneth B. Clark wrote:

> Within the Methodist body, two separate denominations have existed; one, the Negro Central Jurisdiction, is now a matter

of considerable embarrassment to liberal white Methodists who led a "kneel in" at the 1964 General Conference to try to stir the denomination's conscience to prompter action. The vote was to abolish the Central Jurisdiction over the three-year transfer period. Some Negro Methodists have and will continue to resist its abolition just because the parallel Negro hierarchy makes possible Negroes' achievement of power. But in 1964, two Negroes were chosen as bishops, among the forty-four in the Methodist Church, to serve integrated jurisdictions, one, Bishop Prince A. Taylor, Jr., of New Jersey; the other, Bishop James Thomas of Iowa.[11]

Bishop Taylor was not elected in 1964. He was elected in 1956, had served in Liberia for eight years, and had returned to receive this new assignment.

The Central Jurisdictional Conference

On June 17, 1964, the seventh session of the Central Jurisdictional Conference convened at Bethune-Cookman College in Daytona Beach, Florida. One of the visitors present was Charles C. Parlin, who had been chair both of the Commission to Study the Jurisdictional System and the Commission on Interjurisdictional Relations.

After the organization of Committees and other preliminary business, the Jurisdictional Conference turned to the report of the Central Jurisdiction Study Committee. I presented the report as Chair of the Committee. When the issue of realignment of conferences was presented, a motion was made to refer this item to the Committee on Boundaries. The motion to refer was defeated.

There was another amendment:

That the Jurisdictional Conference enact enabling legislation granting authority to any two annual conferences within the same REGIONAL JURISDICTION to merge and form a single annual conference, provided the boundaries of the new conference shall coincide with the geographical boundaries of that JURISDICTION.[12]

This amendment, made by M. J. Jones, was accepted by the Committee.

A later motion, to defer action on the plan for realignment, was defeated. With little additional debate, the report of the Committee to Study the Central Jurisdiction, entitled "Bridges to Racial Equality in the Methodist Church," was accepted by the seventh session of the Central Jurisdictional Conference.

The next important item of business was the election of a general superintendent, with the understanding that he would soon be transferred from the Central to the North Central Jurisdiction. This election continued through sixteen ballots. On the seventeenth ballot, I became the thirteenth bishop to be elected by the Central Jurisdiction.

In its final report to the Jurisdictional Conference, the Committee on Episcopacy made the following assignments for the bishops:

1. Atlantic Coast Area—Bishop M. Lafayette Harris, Residence, Atlanta, Georgia
2. Baltimore Area—Bishop Prince A. Taylor, Jr., Residence, Baltimore, Maryland
3. Chicago Area—Bishop James S. Thomas, Residence, Chicago, Illinois
4. Nashville-Greensboro Area—Bishop Charles F. Golden, Residence, Nashville, Tennessee
5. Southwestern Area—Bishop Noah W. Moore, Residence, Houston, Texas

In a later session of the Jurisdictional Conference, the name of the Nashville-Greensboro Area was changed to the Nashville-Carolina Area.

Because of the previous action to realign annual conferences, it became important to see which annual conferences composed the five areas. This was decided as follows:

Atlantic Coast Area
  Central Alabama
  Florida
  Georgia
  Mississippi
  Upper Mississippi

Baltimore Area
  Delaware
  Washington

Chicago Area
  Lexington

Southwestern Area
  Central West
  Louisiana
  Southwest
  Texas
  West Texas

Nashville-Carolina Area
  Tennessee-Kentucky
  North Carolina-Virginia
  South Carolina

There was still a great deal of territory in two of the Episcopal Areas, but the realignment would make it easier for the white and African American annual conferences to merge.

The Bishops Speak

In the Episcopal Address of 1964, the bishops of the Central Jurisdiction spoke clearly about the ill effects of racial segregation:

> Certainly the sore thumb in our American life is our system of racial segregation. This hydra-headed monster has fared long and succulently upon the irrational prejudices of the blatant minority, and today though weakened, it is still strong and arrogant. It is not only our American sore thumb, it is also our

most vulnerable spot—our Achilles heel, and the most telling attacks upon our church and democratic way of life are aimed at this area. Certainly if anything is wrong and out of harmony with true freedom in a Christian democratic state, it is compulsory or legal segregation, and here the church—our church—does not come into court with clean hands.[13]

Then, following the mood of the General Conference, the Central Jurisdiction bishops said:

Under Amendment IX, provisions have been made for the transfer of churches or conferences from one jurisdiction to another. Some churches have transferred to the North Central, Western, South Central and Northeastern Jurisdictions under this amendment. Conferences in the Central Jurisdiction have been invited to transfer to some of these jurisdictions but to date none has. The hesitancy here has been due to the fact that every conference in the Central Jurisdiction overlaps the geographical area of two or more sectional jurisdictions and the leadership of the jurisdiction feels that no territory in any annual conference ought to be transferred into a jurisdiction in which it did not geographically lie.

The Report of the Committee of Five will come before you early in this session and we know that it will get due consideration at your hands.[14]

Like the General Conference, the bishops of the Central Jurisdiction expected the year of 1964 to be a time for decisive planning and action.

The Transfers of the Delaware and Lexington Annual Conferences

The written record of local church and annual conference transfers must, of necessity, be selective. It is significant to report that a certain act took place on a certain date, but it is perhaps of higher significance to report the many human dramas behind the act.

Knowing that I would be transferring, with the Lexington

Annual Conference, into the North Central Jurisdiction, I did not move to Chicago. Instead, I tried to get the Lexington Conference ready for transfer. Fiscal accounts had to be made ready for a transfer, property matters had to be adjusted, and the membership of the Lexington Conference had to be encouraged to enter this new world with grace and dignity. Then I went to the session of the North Central Jurisdictional Conference meeting in Cleveland, Ohio, July 8-12, 1964.

On Thursday morning, July 9, 1964, the plan, which was carefully worked out in numerous consultations, was presented to the North Central Jurisdictional Conference by Leonard Slutz of Ohio. Mr. Slutz reported that the plan had received 5,746 positive votes in the Conferences of the North Central Jurisdiction and only 9 negative votes. He also indicated that the Central Jurisdiction had taken all the necessary steps prior to transfer. When the plan was presented for a vote by the North Central Jurisdictional Conference the vote was 370 for, none against. The audience stood and sang "Praise God from Whom All Blessings Flow." Legally the Lexington Conference, by that act, ceased to be an Annual Conference of the Central Jurisdiction.

Just after the vote was taken, Bishop Richard C. Raines rose to speak. He began by saying:

> There are certain moments in the long and fruitful history of The Methodist Church that stand out as Mount Everest does on the horizon of our history. Some of them are composed of unalloyed joy and others are shaded with the shadow of sadness and incompleteness.[15]

Bishop Raines continued: "It is one thing to talk about history; it is another thing to make it. You have just done that and now we ratify and welcome that which future historians of The Methodist Church will be writing about and talking about."[16]

He then presented me to the North Central Jurisdiction Conference. And so, on July 9, 1964, I ceased to be a bishop of the Central Jurisdiction and became a bishop of the North Central Jurisdiction. Approximately two weeks earlier, Bishop Prince A. Taylor, Jr., ceased to be a bishop of the Central Jurisdiction and became a bishop of the Northeastern Jurisdiction.

It carries us a little beyond the story of the Central Jurisdiction to report that Bishop Taylor was assigned to the New Jersey Area of the Northeastern Jurisdiction; I was assigned to the Iowa Area of the North Central Jurisdiction.

Amendment IX had finally been used in a highly significant way. The Central Jurisdiction had seen the transfer of two of its most historic annual conferences. This certainly sent a message that was heard throughout the church.

NOTES

1. Episcopal Address, *The Daily Christian Advocate*, April 27, 1964, p. 15.
2. *The Daily Christian Advocate,* April 28, 1964, p. 37.
3. Ibid., p. 145.
4. Ibid.
5. Ibid., p. 161.
6. Ibid., p. 165.
7. "Bridges to Racial Equality," Report to the Central Jurisdictional Conference, June 16–21, 1964, Central Jurisdiction Study Committee, p. 1.
8. Ibid., pp. 15 and 16.
9. Ibid., p. 21.
10. Ibid., p. 27.
11. Kenneth B. Clark, *Dark Ghetto* (New York: Harper & Row, 1965), p. 181.
12. *Journal of the Seventh Session of the Central Jurisdictional Conference of The Methodist Church,* 1964, vol. 7, p. 61.
13. Ibid., p. 117.
14. Ibid., p. 121.
15. North Central Jurisdictional Conference of The Methodist Church, *The Daily Christian Advocate*, July 10, 1964. p. 11.
16. Ibid.

The Merger of
Annual Conferences

The ninety-fifth session of the Lexington Annual Conference was held in Chicago, Illinois, June 10-14, 1964. When the Conference opened, the ministers and lay persons knew that this would be their last session as the Lexington Annual Conference. It was not long before a resolution was presented to the Annual Conferences. It was a Plan for the Merger of the Lexington Annual Conference with the Annual Conferences of the North Central Jurisdiction.

Whereas, it is the avowed policy of the Methodist Church to effect ultimately the dissolution of the Central Jurisdiction as one step toward achieving a truly inclusive Methodist Church, and whereas, the Central and North Central Jurisdictional Conferences and their constituent Annual Conferences are committed to the elimination of all forms of racial segregation and discrimination in the Methodist Church, including elimination, within a framework of overall planning, of the racially segregated Central Jurisdiction itself,

Be It Resolved, therefore that

1—The Lexington Annual Conference in accordance with Amendment IX of the Constitution of the Methodist Church, by adoption of this plan votes to transfer from the Central Jurisdiction to the North Central Jurisdiction.[1]

The preparation of this Plan of Merger was an emotional moment for members of the Lexington Annual Conference.

The presenter of the plan quoted from Leonard Slutz's statement when he presented the Plan of Merger to the North Central Jurisdictional Conference.

> May I say this required five steps. The Lexington Conference has voted overwhelmingly. The other annual conferences of the Central Jurisdiction have done likewise. The annual conferences of the North Central Jurisdiction have taken their action. We have just tabulated the votes in the annual conferences of the North Central Jurisdiction. The votes in favor of this plan across the Conferences of the North Central Jurisdiction were 5,746 as against 9 negative votes.[2]

The members of the ninety-fifth and last session of the Lexington Annual Conference were quite aware of the resolution which was before them. The presenter of the resolution again quoted Leonard Slutz:

> I add just two brief points: four score and fifteen years ago there was created in our country one of the great annual conferences of the Methodist Church. In March of 1869, meeting in Lexington, Kentucky, the Lexington Conference was organized, and it has had a bright and brilliant history.
>
> Some may think that in the next few minutes that great Conference will come to an end, but I submit to you that such is not the case. I say that the great Ohio River does not end at Cairo, Illinois, but rather it there joins with the Mississippi to form an even greater and more powerful stream, so that the waters of those two great rivers together flow onward toward the sea.[3]

These quotations from Leonard Slutz spoke the minds and hearts of many who attended the last session of the Lexington Annual Conference. Yet there was profound sadness as well.

When the Committee on Courtesy made its report, there were words of appreciation for all who had contributed to the Annual Conference session. Then the report ended on this note:

> And now, with golden memories and deepest gratitude for these 95 years of consecrated service as the Lexington Conference, with tender hearts and high hopes for the future, we say our last
> "God be with you till we meet again" as a Lexington Conference.
> FAREWELL! FAREWELL! FAREWELL![4]

On this bittersweet note of knowing the past, but with some fears about the future, the final session of the Lexington Conference came to an end.

The report of the Committee on Social and Economic Relations reflected some of the deep concern and uncertainty of the Lexington Annual Conference in its final session. A part of that report stated:

> The next Quadrennium will probably see the elimination of the Central Jurisdiction as a separate entity. However, the elimination of the Central Jurisdiction will not in itself remove the problem of which segregation is the symbol. Dr. James P. Brawley has suggested two major steps toward the solution of the problem. "The first step is desegregation. It is imperative that the General Conference declare in unequivocal terms that the Church is desegregated, and that no door shall be closed to anyone on the basis of race or color."
> "The second major step is one of programming and changing structure wherever necessary to create the climate of all levels of the Church in which an inclusive Church may be achieved."
> The problems relative to achieving an inclusive Church, to the abolition of the Central Jurisdiction, and the realignment of Conference Boundaries and its effects upon the ministers and laity are tremendous ones.[5]

The remainder of the report of the Committee on Social and Economic Relations was a strong statement in support of the Civil Rights bill that was at that time before the United States Senate.

The Schedule of Merger

In a study of Central Jurisdiction data, Douglas W. Johnson presents an interesting table showing the dates when Central Jurisdiction Conferences were merged with geographic conferences. The Delaware, Washington, and Lexington annual conferences were merged with geographic annual conferences in 1964. The next year, 1965, the Central West Annual Conference of the Central Jurisdiction was merged with geographic annual conferences. With four of its seventeen annual conferences merged with geographic annual conferences, the remaining thirteen annual conferences of the Central Jurisdiction were engaged in various stages of consultation and planning with a view to merger.

Douglas Johnson's data show that mergers took place in every succeeding year from 1968 to the year 1973. His data, taken from the General Minutes of the Methodist Church, reveal how quickly other annual conferences followed the Delaware and the Lexington Annual Conferences.

It is important to note that some annual conferences of the Central Jurisdiction continued to exist as racial annual conferences after the Central Jurisdiction held its last special session in 1967. When The United Methodist Church was formed in 1968, it would have been correct to say that there was no longer a Central Jurisdiction. But, as the table below clearly shows, some racial annual conferences still existed within predominantly white areas.

DATES WHEN CENTRAL JURISDICTION CONFERENCES
MERGED WITH GEOGRAPHIC CONFERENCES
THE UNITED METHODIST CHURCH

Central Jurisdiction Conference	Year Merged
Delaware, Lexington, Washington, D.C.........	1964
Central West..	1965
Tennessee-Kentucky, North Carolina-Virginia..	1968
Florida...	1969
Gulf Coast (Texas), West Texas....................	1970
Louisiana..	1971
Georgia, South Carolina, Southwest.............	1972
Central Alabama, Upper Mississippi, Mississippi...	1973

Source: *General Minutes of The United Methodist Church 1964–1974*[6]

A decade had passed since the annual conference transfers began in 1964.

A Case Study

During the decade between 1964 and 1973, every remaining Central Jurisdiction Annual Conference, through their leaders, was involved in consultations and negotiations leading to merger. One example is the West Texas Annual Conference.

In 1968, at its ninety-fourth annual session, the West Texas Annual Conference received a report from its Inter-Jurisdictional Relations Committee. The resolution stated, in part:

Whereas, all of the Annual Conferences formerly part of the Central Jurisdiction have been transferred and are now part of the South Central Jurisdiction, and

Whereas, the Plan of Union as well as the desire and intent of the Methodist Church has for many years called for the merger of Conferences occupying the same geographical boundaries without regard to race and color at the earliest possible date, and

Whereas, through both Conference and State Committees, representatives of all Conferences involved, have been involved in conversations and plans for merger since 1964, and

Whereas, the financial responsibilities and obligations of all Conferences involved have been carefully considered and reasonable solutions found for most problems.[7]

The resolution continued with specific references to certain bishops and areas. It concluded:

5. By the adoption of this resolution by all the Conferences concerned, namely the Conferences of Bishop Martin's Area, and the Texas Conference of Bishop Moore's Area, the Southwest Texas, the North Texas, the Central Texas and the West Texas Conferences, will be a request to the South Central Jurisdiction, to approve the merger of all Conferences in the State of Texas having overlapping boundaries.

The following is a report of the action taken by the West Texas Annual Conference.[8]

Number of members of the Annual Conference present and eligible to vote: 103.
Number of abstentions   0
Number voting for   102
Number voting against   1

In its ninety-sixth and final session, the West Texas Annual Conference of the Central Jurisdiction presented a detailed plan of merger. The third point of the resolution reflected all of the earlier work done in consultations and negotiations. It was resolved:

That all details of the mergers shall be worked out as rapidly as feasible by consultation between the West Texas Conference and each Annual Conference involved, and that the effective time of the mergers shall be the conclusion of the 1970 Session of the West Texas Conference. It is understood that the consumation (sic) with any one of these conferences shall be contingent upon a satisfactory acceptance by all of the Annual Conferences involved.[9]

The resolution went on to provide for such concerns as property, pension responsibilities, minimum salary, and the support of the one African American college formerly supported by the West Texas Annual Conference.

In two of the Annual Conferences of the Central Jurisdiction it was a matter of relatively easy realignment. Both the South Carolina Annual Conference of the Central Jurisdiction and the South Carolina Conference of the Southeastern Jurisdiction covered the same territory, the entire state. This was also true of the Florida Conferences of the two jurisdictions, except for that part of Florida that belonged to the Alabama-West Florida Annual Conference of the Southeastern Jurisdiction.

All of this required painstaking work. Committees had to be appointed to care for such important matters as property, pensions, and the status of pastors. The task was all the more delicate and difficult when it is remembered that these negotiations brought together people who were not accustomed to working together on any project of church-wide proportions.

To aid the merging annual conferences, the General Conference set up the Temporary General Aid Fund in 1964. The purpose of this fund was to aid annual conferences to pay the same retirement rate to African American pastors who came from annual conferences paying a much lower rate.

Simply to state the years when the Central Jurisdiction

Annual Conferences merged with geographic annual conferences is to miss the real story of human involvement in the mergers. There were the human dramas of committee work, knowing that there was no way to solve the dilemma of segregation either by maintaining the status quo or by going back to business as usual. In some places there was all the delicateness of frayed nerves, distrust, and a longing of some in Central Jurisdiction for the comfortable ways of Central Jurisdiction living.

Now, however, there was no way to go back. As long as it seemed to take in the deep South, it became clear that merger was high on the agenda of the annual conferences and their bishops.

There were times when those of us who had gone into earlier transfers and mergers were called upon to visit other annual conferences, to preach, to consult with committees, and to suggest ways out of specific dilemmas. For a quarter of a century, The Methodist Church had an unbroken structure known as the Central Jurisdiction. It was a dilemma that had to be resolved. In 1964, by the use of Amendment IX of the Constitution of The Methodist Church, the first annual conference transfers were made. Beginning that year and ending with the Central Alabama, Upper Mississippi, and Mississippi Annual Conferences in 1973, all of the Central Jurisdiction Annual Conferences were transferred into geographic annual conferences.

NOTES

1. *Official Journal of the Ninety-fifth Session of the Lexington Annual Conference,* June 10-14, 1964, pp. 46-47.
2. Ibid., p. 47.
3. Ibid.
4. Ibid., p. 55.
5. Ibid., p. 58.
6. Douglas W. Johnson, "A Study of Former Central Jurisdiction Church Data,"

Nation Mission Resources, General Board of Global Ministries, The United Methodist Church, 1987, p. 5.

7. *Journal of the West Texas Conference of The United Methodist Church*, Ninety-fourth Annual Session, May 27-30, 1968, p. 75.

8. Ibid., p. 76.

9. *Journal of the West Texas Conference*, The United Methodist Church, 1970 Session, pp. 77-78.

The Final Session of the
Central Jurisdictional Conference

The eighth session of the Central Jurisdictional Conference—a special session—convened in Nashville, Tennessee, August 17-19, 1967. This session was authorized by the special session of the General Conference meeting in 1966. That special session provided that:

> If before the Uniting Conference of 1968 there shall be one or more vacancies in the College of Bishops of the Central Jurisdiction of the Methodist Church, upon the Plan of Union being adopted by the requisite vote in the Annual Conferences of the Evangelical United Brethren Church and of the Methodist Church, the Central Jurisdiction shall be entitled at a special session to elect to fill the vacancy or vacancies.[1]

The purposes of this special session of the Central Jurisdictional Conference were more clear and limited than usual. Three specific purposes were stated. They were:

> 1. Bringing the affairs of the Central Jurisdiction to an orderly close prior to its dissolution upon the union of The Methodist church and the Evangelical United Brethren Church; and
> 2. The election of a bishop (or bishops) to fill the vacancy (or vacancies) in the College of Bishops of the Central Jurisdiction that exist(s) prior to the Uniting Conference of 1968; and
> 3. The assignment of the bishop (or bishops) of the jurisdiction to their respective residences in accordance with

the provision of Paragraph No. 526 of the 1964 Discipline of
The Methodist Church.[2]

The secretary of the Jurisdictional Conference, Allen M.
Mayes, recognized the historic nature of this final Central
Jurisdictional Conference. In the secretary's foreword he
said:

> I have endeavored to give a true, accurate, and sometimes full
> account of all of the official proceedings and actions of the
> Conference. Because of the historical significance of this
> session of the Jurisdictional Conference, an effort has been
> made to include a record of all addresses, resolutions, and
> speeches.[3]

The secretary of the Jurisdictional Conference knew that
this final session would be memorable in more ways than one.

The Bishops Speak

In earlier episcopal messages the bishops of the Central
Jurisdiction spoke to a full range of topics. This final episcopal
address, however, centered upon the issues of race and
history.
In the foreword the bishops stated:

> This address is an attempt to give a general updating of where
> we are in our efforts to achieve racial inclusiveness in The
> Methodist Church and to call attention to some of the more
> serious aspects of the unfinished task to which the church has
> committed itself and towards which it must continue to move
> as expeditiously as an orderly and thoroughly planned
> transition can be perfected.[4]

Also, to be sure that their message would be understood in
historical context, the bishops called upon two scholars of the
Central Jurisdiction to read papers. Bishop Willis J. King

read a paper on "The Central Jurisdiction, The Methodist Church, 1939–1967."

The bishops went on to write about "Our Heritage," "Socio-cultural Factors of Racism," "Black Americans in the Methodist Church," "Participation in the Mainstream of Methodism," and "The Unfinished Task."

Going back to the Episcopal Address of 1944, they quoted Bishop Alexander P. Shaw, who wrote:

> We are not at all in harmony with any Methodist or others who think such a plan (The Central Jurisdiction) necessary in a truly Christian brotherhood. We consider it expedient only on account of the Christian childhood of some American Methodists who need a little coddling until they can grow into full-grown manhood and womanhood in Christ Jesus.[5]

The bishops reminded this final session of the Central Jurisdictional Conference that "seventeen of the nineteen Negro Annual Conferences voted overwhelmingly against the creation of the Central Jurisdiction as a racial structure on the conviction that this action was morally incompatible with the Christian gospel of oneness in Christ."[6]

As a part of the unfinished task, the bishops called upon the eighth Central Jurisdictional Conference to "set in motion a resolution for a constitutional amendment designed to remove the veto power granted to the Annual Conference in Division Two, Section VII, Paragraph 39, Article VI of the new constitution of The United Methodist Church."[7] The paragraph referred to provided that "For a period of twelve years following union, Annual Conferences shall not have their names of boundaries changed without their consent."

The bishops found it significant that the hotel in which they were meeting was named for Andrew Jackson. They also found it significant that the fourteenth and last bishop elected by the Central Jurisdiction would be consecrated in

McKendree Church, formerly a church of the Methodist Episcopal Church, South.

The Lessons of History

The paper read by Bishop Willis J. King was an excellent review of the "History of the Negro in the Methodist Church Prior to 1939." Among other things, Bishop King pointed out that

> to properly appraise the Central Jurisdiction in The Methodist Church, one cannot begin with the structural arrangement set up in 1939 to accommodate the 300,000 Negro Methodists in The Methodist Church, but must see it as a symbol of the past and present history of the Negro during the nearly two centuries of its existence in America.[8]

Among the facts reported by Bishop King were these:

• In 1847, the Methodist Episcopal Church, South reported 124,961 African American members. The membership grew to 127,241 in 1848. Growth continued to 146,949 in 1853 and to 171,857 in 1860. But by 1866, probably for many and complex reasons, the African American membership of the Methodist Episcopal Church, South had shrunk to 78,742.

• By 1850, the total enrollment of African Americans in the Methodist Episcopal Church was 26,309. This was in great contrast even to the lowest recorded membership of African Americans in the Methodist Episcopal Church, South during the same period.

• The Mississippi Mission Conference, composed of both white and African American members, was organized in New Orleans, Louisiana, December 25, 1865, with four districts: one in Mississippi, two in Louisiana, and one in Texas.

• By the close of the 1872–1876 quadrennium, twenty

conferences, white, African American, and mixed, had been organized on the border and in the South.

"By 1895, mixed Annual Conferences, composed of both white and African American ministers, no longer existed in the Methodist Church."[9]

These facts, little known or remembered by members of the last Central Jurisdictional Conference, provided perspective.

If mixed conferences of African Americans and whites existed once, it would not be entirely strange for them to exist again.

For his part, Dr. James P. Brawley addressed the subject: The Central Jurisdiction, The Methodist Church, 1939–1967. He began by describing "The Problem of Race."

> The Central Jurisdiction came into being as a reflection of the long existing race problem in The Methodist Church. The race problem has been present since the establishment of the first Methodist societies, and has been a vital issue from the organization of the church in 1784 to the present.[10]

Brawley reminded the members of the eighth Central Jurisdictional Conference of the growth of the Central Jurisdictional Conferences. "Negro delegations," he said, "were present in every General Conference from 1868 to 1936."

Other little-known facts were made known to the Central Jurisdictional Conference of 1967.

• A strong statement on race was adopted by the General Conference as early as 1944. Among other things, this statement said: "We believe that God is Father of all peoples and races, Jesus Christ is his Son, that we and all men are brothers, and that man is of infinite worth as a Child of God."[11]

The General Conference Committee on Race, in its report to the General Conference of 1948, made specific reference to the Central Jurisdiction.

> Minority groups in The Methodist Church feel keenly the pressure of segregation through provisional Annual Conferences for minority groups and in the Central Jurisdiction in which Negroes are concerned. . . . The Central Jurisdiction is tantamount to a segregated Negro Church within the framework of The Methodist Church. . . .[12]

Brawley continued his address by pointing out that the 1948 General Conference directed the bishops to appoint a Committee to Study the Field of Social Action. The Committee was appointed and made its report in 1952. Out of this action came the Board of Social and Economic Relations which existed from 1952 to 1960.

Reference has already been made to Amendment IX of the Constitution of The Methodist Church. This amendment was ratified by the Annual Conferences in 1958. When the Report of the Commission of Seventy recommended "no basic change in the Central Jurisdiction," the African American members of the General Conference were sadly disappointed.

Turning from General Conference actions to the Central Jurisdiction, James P. Brawley reported how the Central Jurisdiction sought solutions of its own.

A Special Study Committee was appointed by the Central Jurisdictional Conference of 1948. Among the important facts reported to the Central Jurisdiction Conference of 1952 were these:

• The Central Jurisdiction's racial problem needed to be seen "in the light of Christian and democratic concepts."

• From 1928 to 1951 General Board members elected as jurisdictional representatives increased from 40 to 101. Episcopal representation increased from three to six.[13]

• Church membership in the 19 Annual Conferences of the Jurisdiction increased from 317,790 in 1930 to 345,204 in 1950, a total gain in twenty years of only 33,854.[14]

• With reference to the Central Jurisdiction a majority of

both laypersons and ministers responding to questions thought that there should be no segregation in any form, and that the Central Jurisdiction should be eliminated.[15]

The Central Jurisdictional Conference of 1952 continued a Special Study Committee to study its place in The Methodist Church. When the Committee made its report in 1956, it said, among other things:

> While the Central Jurisdiction has been the focal point of attack, it should be made clear that *the major problem of The Methodist Church with reference to race relations is segregation.* It is possible to have segregation without the Central Jurisdiction, and it is possible to have desegregation without its abolition.[16]

The Central Jurisdiction did not have a Study Committee during the quadrennium 1956–1960. The leaders of the Central Jurisdiction did not want to duplicate or have conflict with the General Conference Commission to study the jurisdictional system.

While few of these facts may have been remembered by the members of the Central Jurisdictional Conference, in that final session they could look back over the years and see the journey over which they had come. Among the summary facts and positions set forth by Willis J. King and James P. Brawley were these:

1) The problem of the Central Jurisdiction had long and deep historical roots. The Central Jurisdiction was simply a later expression of the race problem in the United States.

2) The numerical growth of the Central Jurisdiction was slight—a total gain of only 33,854 in twenty years.

3) The Methodist Church had experience with mixed Annual Conferences, if only for a brief time.

4) As early as 1944 the General Conference had before it strong statements on race, some of them specifically mentioning the Central Jurisdiction.

5) As early as 1948, the Central Jurisdiction had Special Study Commissions. This was true of every quadrennium except 1956–1960. During this quadrennium the leaders of the Central Jurisdiction thought that they could rely upon the work of the General Conference Commission on Interjurisdictional Relations.

6) When the Commission on Interjurisdictional Relations, in its report to the 1960 General Conference, recommended that there be no change in the status of the Central Jurisdiction, the Central Jurisdictional Conference requested its bishops to choose a Committee of Five persons, one from each area.

One of the tasks of the Committee of Five was to: "explore the procedures for seeking consensus within the Central Jurisdiction with respect to achieving the goal of an inclusive Methodist Church at all levels of church life."[17]

With this kind of perspective, the Central Jurisdiction turned to the work of its final session.

Message from the Council of Bishops

Because the president of the Council of Bishops, Donald Tippett, could not be present, Bishop Dwight E. Loder came to the final session of the Central Jurisdictional Conference representing the Council of Bishops. In his address to the Conference Bishop Loder said:

> The call is to shatter at once a national symbol of segregation in the church. This is happening here. This is only one step—but under God it is a step. We must move beyond this with dispatch to shatter all that separates us within the Christian Fellowship, on the Annual Conference and local parish level. We must destroy the remainder of personal racial prejudice. If we are Christian—we cannot do less. This will happen—it cannot be stopped.[18]

Bishop Loder's address was delivered near the end of the Central Jurisdictional Conference on Friday afternoon, August 18, 1967.

Election of a Bishop

On August 17, 1967, the Committee on Episcopacy made report number 3 to the Jurisdictional Conference. It recommended that one bishop be elected and set the time for the casting of ballots for Friday morning, August 18, 1967.

The report on ballot number one showed votes for seven persons. There was no election. On the second ballot L. Scott Allen received the necessary two-thirds of the votes and was declared elected. He became the fourteenth and last bishop to be elected by the Central Jurisdiction.

Transition

Knowing that transfers of annual conferences would continue, the eighth session of the Central Jurisdictional Conference elected a Transitional Trustee Board. This trustee board was composed of three bishops, the Jurisdictional Conference secretary, the Jurisdictional Conference treasurer, and one member from each of ten annual conferences.

The duties of this transitional Trustee Board were:

To transfer and dispose of the property of the Jurisdiction as the conference may determine; to care for such practical and legal matters as may be necessary in the phasing out of the Jurisdiction; and to do all things necessary and in the interests of all Annual Conferences of the Jurisdiction as such interests relate to the dissolution and phasing out of the Central Jurisdiction.[19]

This trustee board would have much work to do. The next year, 1968, two of the southern annual conferences of the

Central Jurisdiction would merge with geographic areas. The Tennessee-Kentucky Annual Conference and the North Carolina-Virginia Annual Conferences merged with the white annual conferences of the states in which they were located.

On Saturday morning, August 19, 1967, L. Scott Allen was consecrated as the fourteenth and last bishop elected by the Central Jurisdiction. After an impressive worship service the Central Jurisdiction of The Methodist Church became a part of the history of the church.

Upon the adjournment of the final session of the Central Jurisdictional Conference, the place of major action in race relations shifted to the geographical jurisdictions and the Areas of The Methodist Church. It would take these jurisdictions and Areas six years to complete all of the mergers and transfers but the Advisory Councils of each annual conference continued their work, even in the deep South.

From the time that the Central Jurisdiction was written into the Constitution of The Methodist Church to the time of its final session, twenty-eight years had passed. Even though all but two of the African American Annual Conferences had voted against the Central Jurisdiction, there were mixed feelings during its last session. Old friendship networks would now have to give way to new ways of thinking and acting. The future was not at all clear, but on August 20, 1967, all members of the Central Jurisdiction knew that there was no way back to the structure that had now gone out of existence.

NOTES

1. Special Session of the General Conference, *The Daily Christian Advocate*, November 12, 1966, p. 923.
2. *Journal of the Eighth Session of the Central Jurisdictional Conference*, p. 7.
3. Ibid., p. 9.

4. Ibid., p. 69.
5. Ibid., p. 74.
6. Ibid.
7. Ibid.
8. Ibid., p. 103.
9. Ibid., p. 108.
10. Ibid., p. 120.
11. Ibid., p. 124.
12. Quadrennial Report, 1948; original Report of the Commission, III, "Problems Attendant Upon Organization," p. 7.
13. *Journal of the Eighth Session of the Central Jurisdictional Conference*, p. 129.
14. Ibid.
15. Ibid.
16. Ibid., p. 130.
17. Charles F. Golden and James S. Thomas, *Central Jurisdiction Speaks*, p. 6.
18. Ibid., p. 113.
19. Ibid., p. 48.

11

An Appraisal

F rom the beginning the Central Jurisdiction was controversial. Its inclusion in the Plan of Union was seen differently by the majority of white Methodists, who voted for it, and the majority of African American Methodists, who voted against it.

Given the predominant attitudes then existing in race relations, the Central Jurisdiction "made sense" to many of those who wanted to achieve Methodist Union. One of Methodism's great bishops of that time, Bishop Edwin Holt Hughes, spoke for the white majority when he said: "Our commission on Church Union was not to remake the Church, but to reunite it. We were compelled to resist the good radicals who tried to slip into the government of the union Church provision for their favorite theories."[1]

If the Central Jurisdiction made sense to many of those who wanted Methodist Union in 1939, why did it not also make sense to African American leaders and annual conferences?

The answer to that question can be found in the very different ways in which African American and white leaders viewed the church in 1939. Bishop Hughes was right in saying that The Methodist Church had always had Negro annual conferences. As we have seen, separate African American annual conferences had existed since 1868. And before that there were separate African American mission conferences. Except for brief periods of time, when there were mixed annual conferences, there was no record of integration of annual conferences and local churches.

That was not the issue for African American leaders. The issue was whether or not The Methodist Church could think and act differently in 1939 than it did a half century earlier. The majority of white leaders of The Methodist Church considered church union to be a goal that simply had to be achieved without, as Bishop Hughes put it, "remaking the Church." By their votes, the majority of the African American leaders wanted the church to be remade in many ways, but certainly as far as racial inclusion was concerned.

In all fairness, it must be said that there was more ambivalence among African Americans than their negative votes and abstentions would indicate. One of the great African American leaders spoke for the compromise implicit in the Plan of Union. Matthew Simpson Davage made it clear that he was for the Plan of Union as one step toward "the ultimate goal of one fold and one Shepherd. . . ."[2]

For many African Americans, the Central Jurisdiction, once it became a fact, did provide opportunities that The Methodist Church was willing to give at that time. One of these was disproportionate representation on boards and agencies of the church. This was not asked for by African American leaders but, once given, it did provide an opportunity for closer contact with higher levels of The Methodist Church than was possible prior to Methodist Union.

In retrospect, it is possible to see how the Central Jurisdiction represented both a dilemma and an opportunity. Many African American leaders resented the rationalization that "the Central Jurisdiction is good for you to develop your own leadership." Nevertheless, it is a fact that African American leadership did develop in the Central Jurisdiction, often under adverse circumstances. Could it be possible that the Central Jurisdiction was both a dilemma and an opportunity?

In 1964 I wrote an article in which I made the statement

that the Central Jurisdiction was an opportunity for The Methodist Church to become the inclusive church that it did not become in 1939. Among other things, I said:

> The existence of the Central Jurisdiction within the structure of The Methodist Church is a theological and sociological fact of formidable proportions. Its existence constitutes both the present dilemma and greatest possible opportunity of The Methodist Church. When a nation and a denomination are committed to principles which are difficult to express in practice, they face a dilemma. The alternatives are almost too simple to state: get rid of the principles or get rid of the problem.[3]

If the Central Jurisdiction, as a structure, became a setting in which African Americans could have more contact with the wider church, it was, no less, a setting in which The Methodist Church could, after a quarter of a century, show to itself and to others a more excellent way.

In earlier chapters, the attempt was made to state and interpret the facts and moods of the Central Jurisdiction and the wider church during the years between 1939 and 1967. This final chapter presents the opportunity to reflect upon the Central Jurisdiction in a more personal way.

The story of the Central Jurisdiction is more, much more, than a recital of facts. It is a story of hot debates and at least a few statesmanlike efforts to make the most of the racial structure while it existed. It is also a story of ambivalence, of the straightforward presentation of the ideal and a practical reliance upon the real.

It would require a much larger volume to tell the story in greater detail. The gatherings of people who traveled hundreds of miles to get to a pastors' school, the network of friends made and kept as members of the Central Jurisdiction stayed in each others' homes, the little controversies over live issues of mission and ministry—all of these are part of a story that needs to be told.

This chapter will reflect upon the membership, leadership, institutions, ministry, and the Committee of Five. It will be one person's view of the stories within the story.

Membership

The membership of the Central Jurisdiction never reached 375,000. In the year 1940, the membership of the Central Jurisdiction was 359,860. Three years after that, in 1943, the membership decreased to 320,600. This was the lowest recorded total membership of the Central Jurisdiction over the twenty-seven years of its existence with all of its Annual Conferences.

For thirteen years (1940–52) the *General Minutes of The Methodist Church* provided a column for inactive membership. These figures are significant because they reveal the actual number of persons who were active participants in the membership of local churches in the Central Jurisdiction. Of the 359,860 total members in the Central Jurisdiction in 1940, 51,283 were recorded as inactive. The table below will show how the membership of the Central Jurisdiction fluctuated from one quadrennium to another.

Year	Total Active Membership	Inactive
1940	309,577	51,283
1944	282,654	64,422
1948	262,767	77,012
1952	273,358	73,695

Source: *General Minutes of The Methodist Church*

After the year 1952, the *General Minutes* recorded only the total membership figures.

The total membership of the Central Jurisdiction at the end of each of the later quadrennia is shown in the following table:

Year	Total Membership
1952	347,053
1956	352,972
1960	367,340
1964	373,595

(Source: *General Minutes of The Methodist Church*)

The difference between the lowest recorded membership in 1943 and the highest in 1964 (373,595) is 52,995 members.

There are several ways in which these membership figures can be interpreted. One of these ways is to look at the years of significant increases. After recording its lowest membership in 1943, 320,600, the Central Jurisdiction reported a significant increase the next year: from 320,600 in 1943 to 346,600 in 1944. This was an increase of 25,476 members. That seems to be good. But after recording this increase between 1943 and 1944, the record shows a decrease for the following year: from 346,076 in 1944 to 328,371 in 1945. This is a decrease of 17,705.

Perhaps the safest generalization to offer on the membership of the Central Jurisdiction is that the membership fluctuated between years and quadrennia, never falling below 320,000 and never rising above 374,000.

It is significant to note that during the last decade of the existence of the Central Jurisdiction, the membership grew in more stable ways.

In 1940 the Jurisdictional membership was 359,860. The membership did not reach 350,000 again until 1954 when it was 352,107. This was 7,753 fewer members than the 1940 figure of 359,860.

The membership figure for the Central Jurisdiction in 1955 was 359,786. Except for a decrease of 6,814 members in 1956, the total membership of the Central Jurisdiction showed a small but steady increase each year. This is shown in the table below.

Year	Total Membership
1957	361,388
1958	364,689
1959	366,889
1960	367,340
1961	368,485
1962	368,811
1963	373,327
1964	373,595

(Source: *General Minutes of The Methodist Church*)

After the Delaware and Lexington Annual Conferences merged with geographic annual conferences the total remaining membership of the Central Jurisdiction was approximately 240,000.[4]

Leadership

Whether or not the Central Jurisdiction helped African American leadership to develop is a question that cannot be answered. One thing is clear: there were outstanding leaders of the African American annual conferences before 1939. Now we know, in retrospect, that African American leadership also grew after the Central Jurisdiction was abolished in 1967.

In their final Episcopal Address to a Central Jurisdictional Conference, the bishops reminded the Conference of a long line of leaders.

We joyously and proudly relate ourselves to Harry Hoozier, John Stewart—America's first missionary to Indians—Francis Burns, the first missionary Bishop in The Methodist Church, elected in 1858, and a long host of persons remembered by some of us here today and a few who are themselves among us. We think of I. Garland Penn, M. C. B. Mason, W. F. Isaiah, J. W. E. Bowen, Sr., Robert E. Jones, L. H. King, M. W. Clair, Sr., Mary McLeod Bethune, Charles A. Tindley, R. N. Brooks, W. Scott Chinn, W. A. C. Hughes, L. M. McCoy, D. W. Dogan, A. P. Shaw, J. E. Bowen (sic), Jr., D. W. Henry, E. F. Scarbrough, R. M. Williams, J. W. Golden, E. W. Kelly, J. W. Haywood, and M. S. Davage.[5]

The fact that this many names came so readily to mind is itself significant. Even so, this is only a partial list of the leaders of the African American Methodists who guided and inspired the annual conferences both prior to and following the Union of 1939.

Seven of the names in this list were bishops. However, they were recognized leaders before they became bishops. For example, every editor of the *Central Christian Advocate*, and before that name, the *Southwestern Christian Advocate*, eventually became a bishop.

Because the Central Jurisdiction was so vast in its geography, there were leaders who "held things together" until the bishop came or annual conferences convened. In this group were the district superintendents, the Executive Secretaries of Christian Education, and the college presidents. Budget limitations prevented the development of a full corps of leaders for the large and unwieldy geography of the Central Jurisdiction. Each leader had to do many different things.

The district superintendents visited the local churches at least once a quarter. Unfortunately the local church was expected to pay a portion of the salary of the district superintendent during those visits. This practice was not good for the image of a servant ministry, but it went along with the difficulty in coordinating resources and providing a central treasury.

The Executive Secretary of Christian Education was not an executive, in the strict sense of that term. He or she was more of a resource person. It was his or her job to visit local churches on a regular basis to recommend and provide church school material and related resources.

The presidents of the twelve African American colleges were leaders in the Central Jurisdiction. They were expected to visit annual conferences, especially those from which most of the students came. When the time came for the election of delegates to the General and Jurisdictional Conferences, the members of annual conferences very often turned to the college presidents.

Few areas of the Central Jurisdiction could afford administrative assistants to the bishop. For the areas that did have administrative assistants, this leader also became a resource person. At his best, the administrative assistant could help the bishop by his presence and resourcefulness.

Any list of Central Jurisdiction leadership would certainly be longer than that given by the bishops in their final episcopal address to the Central Jurisdictional Conferences. There were a few pastors, like Charles A. Tindley, who led churches with a membership of five thousand members or more.

Since any short list of Central Jurisdiction leaders would be incomplete, I am selecting two laymen whose impact upon the Jurisdiction was strong and lasting.

Matthew Simpson Davage

This preacher's son was named for one of the great bishops of the church, Matthew Simpson. Born in 1879, Dr. Davage became the president of five colleges: Samuel Huston,

George R. Smith, Rust, Clark, and Huston-Tillotson. He was a man of distinguished bearing and great integrity. In 1924, Dr. Davage became the second African American president of Clark College in Atlanta, Georgia. He was the distinguished president of Clark for seventeen years. Then, in 1941, he was elected to the staff of the Board of Education, with particular responsibility for the twelve African American colleges and one seminary. Dr. Davage rendered outstanding service in this position for twelve years. Then, in 1952, at the age of 73, he was elected president—for the fifth time—of the newly-merged Samuel Huston College (Methodist) and Tillotson College (Congregational) in Austin, Texas. In 1955 Dr. Davage retired from that position and made his home in New Orleans, Louisiana.

The education that Matthew Simpson Davage received at New Orleans University served him well. He was not an orator in the old classical meaning of that term. Rather, from a well-furnished mind, he could quote, from memory, poems and statements from ancient and modern sources.

Dr. Davage's leadership was widely recognized, both in the Central Jurisdiction and beyond. At one time the high respect for Dr. Davage in the Central Jurisdiction led a significant group of leaders to inquire as to whether or not they could elect him a bishop.

I succeeded Dr. Davage in the staff of the Board of Education. Since he was a college president again—for the fifth time—he was a member of the Presidents' Council over which I presided. He was unfailingly gracious during the three years of his final presidency.

In 1940, when the Central Jurisdiction became a structural reality, many of the leaders looked to Dr. Davage for the early leadership that was needed. He proved to be equal to the task.

James P. Brawley

The leadership of James P. Brawley came in a quite different style from that of Matthew Simpson Davage. Like Davage, Brawley was a product of one of the African American Methodist Colleges, Samuel Huston College in Austin, Texas. He did graduate work at Northwestern University, from which he received both the Master of Arts and the Doctor of Philosophy degrees.

In the summer of 1926, Brawley became the dean of Clark College in Atlanta. He worked very closely with Matthew Simpson Davage who was the president at that time. His quiet and thorough work as dean complemented Davage's work as the much-traveled president of Clark College.

Like Davage, Brawley was elected to several General Jurisdictional Conferences. He became, as Bishop Prince A. Taylor, Jr., puts it, "one of the architects of the dissolution of the Central Jurisdiction." More than that, the record will show that he was the chief architect of the inclusion of the Central Jurisdiction into the total structure of The Methodist Church.

In 1948, Brawley offered the first resolution calling for a Commission to Study the Central Jurisdiction.

Bishop Taylor described what went on behind the scenes:

> James P. Brawley, then president of Clark College, Atlanta, at the Central Jurisdictional Conference, held at Clark, 1948, offered a resolution that the conference set up a Commission to Study the Jurisdiction. The resolution was adopted and the bishops empowered to name the Commission. A year passed and nothing was done. Dr. Brawley and Prince Taylor met with the College of Bishops in 1949 and urged the bishops to name the Commission. The bishops named Dr. Brawley Chairman and Prince Taylor was named Secretary.[6]

Even though a year of work was lost, Brawley and Taylor produced a thoughtful and carefully written report for the

1952 Central Jurisdictional Conference. Brawley kept the bishops in touch with the work of the commission. He reported for the Commission to the Central Jurisdictional Conference of 1952.

On the basis of their intellectual ability and their character, Davage and Brawley would have been leaders in any age. After Davage retired, in 1955, Brawley continued his leadership in the Central Jurisdiction and in the General Conferences.

Institutions

The major post-secondary educational institutions of the Central Jurisdiction were twelve colleges and one theological seminary. Since hotel accommodations were not open to African Americans until the mid-sixties, the colleges were gathering places for the lay persons and ministers of the Central Jurisdiction. It was on these campuses that institutes and Pastors' Schools were held. Four of the seven Central Jurisdictional Conferences were held on the campuses of African American Methodist Colleges—Bennett, Clark, Dillard, and Bethune Cookman colleges.

These colleges also provided a communication link to the white Annual Conferences of the north. In 1866 an unofficial Freedmen's Aid Society founded many of these colleges. After a time, the colleges received financial support, first through a Lincoln Day offering and later on Race Relations Sunday. The college presidents and choirs would visit white Annual Conferences of the North both to seek more financial support and to report on the progress made by the college during a given year.

The lack of money prevented the acquisition of property that might be used as camp sites or study centers. There was one notable exception. Many years ago, Bishop Robert E. Jones visited Lakeside, Ohio, a beautiful site with homes and camp facilities on Lake Erie. This gave him the inspiration to acquire land for Gulfside. In time this became a beautiful site on the Gulf of Mexico in the state of Mississippi.

Ministry

Ministry, as it is presented in this section, refers to the training, service, and effectiveness of the pastors and district superintendents of the Central Jurisdiction. There are few studies of the ministry of the Central Jurisdiction.

Surprisingly, much of the data on the ministry of the Central Jurisdiction are either statistical, on the one hand, or impressionistic, on the other. The few statistical studies need interpretation and the broadly based impressionistic studies need focus. Ralph A. Felton wrote one of the few studies of the ministry of the Central Jurisdiction that both presents and interprets statistical data.

Unfortunately we do not have a date for the Felton Study. Since he refers to sources written in or near the year 1953, Dr. Felton's Study must have been written in the mid-fifties.

The first finding of Felton's Study was that the districts served by district superintendents of the Central Jurisdiction were considerably smaller than those served by district superintendents in three of the other jurisdictions. When he asked a group of Central Jurisdiction district superintendents, "If additional travel expenses were provided, would you favor the principle of larger districts?"—sixteen of the twenty said "Yes."

There were many reasons for the smaller number of pastoral charges served by Central Jurisdiction district superintendents. Two of these reasons were distance and expense. Felton makes a vital point when he reported that, if more pastoral charges were served, it would have released more persons for the pastorate.

Generally speaking, the ministry of the Central Jurisdiction was marked by low salaries, small church memberships, and a feeling of isolation. While it is true that other jurisdictions also had small churches and low salaries, none was quite so low as those in the Central Jurisdiction.

In 1951, the average annual salary for pastors in the Central Jurisdiction was $1,093. A Jurisdictional picture is given in the table below.

Average Annual Salary Received
by the Pastors in the Different Jurisdictions[7]
(for 1951)

Jurisdiction	Average Salary
North Central	$2,721
Southeastern	2,655
South Central	2,603
Northeastern	2,459
Western	2,455
Central	1,092
Average for the church	$2,485

While these figures for all Jurisdictions seem extremely low for the 1990s, the buying power of a dollar was much greater in the 1950s.

When Felton asked 109 Central Jurisdiction pastors where they lived, fifty-eight or 53.2 percent answered that they owned their own homes. An additional twenty-six or 23.9 percent said they were renting. Only seventeen or 15.6 percent said that they lived in parsonages.[8]

Reflecting the racial attitudes of the South in the midfifties, the pastors reported that 14 of 483 communities in which they served were antagonistic. In 266 communities the pastors felt complete isolation. Of the 483 communities, 266 were described as "paternalistic" on the part of whites.[9]

One of the important studies of African American churches and pastors was published in 1976. This study, by Shockley, Brewer, and Townsend revealed that much of the low morale of African American churches and pastors was present in the early years following the inclusion of the Central Jurisdiction. The authors quote an African American district superintendent who said:

> I don't know. First, the black church is slowly but surely ebbing away. Unless something is hurriedly done to check the backward flow, there will be nothing left to "include." Second, "sensitivity sessions" help a little but their value dies when the majority group becomes at home with the facts so that guilt is no longer felt, then things return to "normal."[10]

This study was published just three years after the inclusion of the last Central Jurisdictional Annual Conference. It would be helpful to have a study made of the attitudes of African American pastors and district superintendents at this date, almost twenty years after all of the Central Jurisdiction Annual Conferences had been included in regional jurisdictions.

The Committee of Five

Over three months after the close of the 1960 Central Jurisdictional Conference, I received a letter from Bishop Edgar A. Love, the Secretary of the College of Bishops. There is no record of what transpired between July 17, 1960, when the Jurisdictional Conference closed, and the date of the letter, November 29, 1960. It may well have been a time of carefully pondering who should be on the Committee of Five and how its major work should be described.

On Saturday, July 16, 1960, James P. Brawley made the

report of the Special Committee to Study Problems in Relation to the Central Jurisdiction. After some discussion, an amendment was offered by Joseph E. Lowery of Alabama:

> That a jurisdictional committee be created for the quadrennium 1960–1964 consisting of five members, one from each area, without regard to orders, appointed by the College of Bishops, to work in conjunction with the Jurisdictional Committee on Christian Social Concerns and the representatives on the Commission on Interjurisdictional Relations, and to study the broader aspects of problems and adjustments. . . .[11]

The amendment was accepted by the Special Committee to Study Problems in relation to the Central Jurisdiction and, later, by the Jurisdictional Conference.

It was in reply to this amendment that Bishop Love wrote to me.

November 29, 1960

Dr. James S. Thomas
Post Office Box 871
Nashville, Tennessee

Dear James,
    This is to advise you that you have been appointed to the Special Committee of Five for Jurisdictional Study, which Committee is to cooperate with the Committee of Dr. James P. Brawley. I am asking you to call this Committee to meet at the earliest convenience. Kindly give Dr. Brawley notice to be present as a member ex-officio. The other members of the Committee are:

> Mr. R. C. Erwin (Baltimore Area)
> 13 East 3rd Street
> Winston-Salem, North Carolina

The Rev. J. H. Graham (Nashville-Birmingham)
1701 Arch Street
Philadelphia, Pennsylvania

Mr. William A. Kirk (New Orleans Area)
(Address to be supplied)

Mr. John J. Hicks, Sr. (St. Louis Area)
208 North Leffingwell Street
St. Louis, Missouri

Sincerely yours,
Edgar A. Love

As soon as it could be arranged, the first meeting of the
Committee was held at Clark College in Atlanta. Dr. James P.
Brawley was present for that first meeting and remained
throughout the session.

Since Bishop Love's letter to me did not mention a
Chairman, I would not presume to be Chairman just because
he asked me to call the first meeting. The first item on the
agenda was the election of a Chairman. When that was done,
the Committee, with the help of Dr. Brawley, spent considerable time in studying the work of predecessor committees.
Careful attention was given to the use of Amendment IX and
some of the reasons why so few churches had transferred to
regional jurisdictions during the preceding quadrennium.

The next item on the agenda was a careful consideration of
what the Committee would do before the next session of the
Jurisdictional Conference. Two items were of immediate
importance. First the Committee was mandated to "Analyze
the proposals, recommendations, and actions of the Commission on Interjurisdictional Relations as they relate or
involve the Central Jurisdiction." Second, "In the first year of
the quadrennium the Committee shall give special attention
to the methods and procedures by which the Central
Jurisdiction may be dissolved."[12]

While it is not known how the persons were chosen to be on the Committee of Five, a rationale very quickly emerged. It is possible that the College of Bishops consulted Dr. Brawley and others before appointing the Committee. However it was done, the selection of the persons to be on the Committee of Five turned out to be a fortunate combination of knowledge and skills.

Richard C. Erwin was a lay person, a lawyer, from North Carolina. He had a thorough knowledge of the *Discipline* and of legal procedures. His commitment to the church was very clear. He participated in the life of the church at every level open to lay persons.

John H. Graham was a minister then serving on the Division of National Missions of the Board of Missions of The Methodist Church. A native of Mississippi, he traveled widely throughout the Central Jurisdiction in his work. He had served his Annual Conference with distinction and was very well acquainted with lay leaders in the Central Jurisdiction.

W. Astor Kirk was a lay person, a former professor of Political Science at Huston-Tillotson College in Austin, Texas. A brilliant student of the workings of voluntary associations, he was also well acquainted with the work of The Methodist Church. At the time of his appointment to the Committee of Five, he was a staff member of the Board of Christian Social Concerns in Washington, D.C.

John J. Hicks was a pastor of one of the most influential local churches in the Central Jurisdiction, Union Memorial in St. Louis. Often sought after as a preacher to special groups, he also possessed a thorough knowledge of the Central Jurisdiction. He is now deceased.

I was a pastor of the South Carolina Conference and traveled throughout the Central Jurisdiction as a fund-raiser and trustee of the twelve African American colleges. I was often called upon to speak and write on the Central Jurisdiction as an issue that needed to be resolved.

This was the Committee of Five: two lay persons, three ministers, among them a lawyer, a former college professor and social researcher, three General Board staff persons, one a pastor of a local church, and, ex-officio, a college president who was the architect of Central Jurisdictional inclusion.

In a group of such varied skills and backgrounds, one could find the great advantage of creative production and the ever-present possibility of strong disagreement. As chairman I considered my role to be an enabler, a planner, a resource person. I also took very seriously the role of one who would move toward consensus when that became necessary—and often it became necessary.

It would require another volume to tell the story of the Committee's work in terms of human dynamics. After our first meeting, we projected a series of dates for future meetings and committed ourselves to the priority of attending each meeting.

Along with the work of the Committee in session, each member had to deal with persistent rumors, many suggestions from interested persons and a few leaders who questioned what we were doing. There were many long distance phone calls, day and night, each coming from an interested person who wanted to offer a contribution.

We tried to take all of these communications as resources, all of them gently prodding us to do our best. There were some interpretations of the Committee's work that were more expressions of concern than resources for improvement.

Some of this part of the Committee's work is illustrated by a letter which came to me from one of our members.

July 3, 1962

Dear Brother Thomas:
    I received a long distance call the other night from a brother in the Central Jurisdiction who was very much enraged. He said that he understood the Committee of Five was

authorized to plan the blueprint for the dissolution of the jurisdiction but he said he understood that you and Kirk were to meet with Mr. Parlin in New York. He asked, "Has Mr. Parlin conquered the Committee? Is he writing the blueprint for the dissolution of the Jurisdiction again?" I called you the same night but was told that you were traveling and could not be reached.[13]

It was very important to inform the writer of the letter that the Jurisdictional Conference had asked the Committee of Five to "analyze the proposals, recommendations, and actions of the Commission on Interjurisdictional Relations as they relate to the Central Jurisdiction." If this was to be done properly, it may—and it did—require face-to-face meetings with the Chairman of the Commission on Interjurisdictional Relations.

The Committee of Five considered it important to communicate with all persons who wanted interpretations of its work. Members of the Committee were invited to many annual conferences to make progress reports and to help in the building of a consensus among those who anticipated the 1964 General and Jurisdictional Conferences.

A minor, but important, part of our work was to respond to some letters instructing us on the importance of the separation of the races. The few who did write such instructions often left no room for a reply; they made statements of such one-sided nature as to require no answer.

The Committee of Five came early to the conclusion that its work was to provide two things that the General Conference Commissions had not been able to provide prior to 1964. The first was a comprehensive and sequential plan by which Amendment IX might be used for the transfer of Annual Conferences of the Central Jurisdiction. The second was a building of consensus, if not trust, within the Central Jurisdiction so that any plan for the inclusion of the Central Jurisdiction would be one toward which the Central

Jurisdiction had made a major contribution. One has only to analyze the debate on the Central Jurisdiction at the General Conference of 1964 to see the importance of these two contributions.

Often it takes the passing of years before any story can be told in historical perspective. It is now important to ask several questions.

First, in the years since the last Central Jurisdictional Annual Conference has been included in regional jurisdictions, what lessons can one learn about the human dynamics of change?

The answer to that question can be long or short. One short answer is that the Central Jurisdiction, a dilemma from the first, revealed again how difficult it is to make lasting social changes. Two of the greatest fears expressed during the debate on Union have failed to materialize. Both were expressed by a bishop of the South who said: "If the churches are united, we will have to accept Negroes in our church. Social equality will be taught in our schools."[14]

An elaboration on this statement is hardly necessary. The plain fact is that there has been no invasion of white churches by African Americans and the term "our church" has been greatly enlarged by the active participation of African Americans.

Second, if the Central Jurisdiction is considered as a case study, how was inclusion finally achieved?

A careful reading of all the General Conference debates on the Central Jurisdiction will reveal a strong appeal to the Christian ideal. Influential leaders made it clear that there are certain things the church should do and be. Over and over it became clear that segregation in a structure of the church was indefensible. Also, there were opportunities for extensive consultation and contacts between African American and white leaders. Strained at first, then gradually more natural, the meeting places and times for white Methodists and African American Methodists provided new perspectives.

Third, in the twenty-nine years since the inclusion of the last Central Jurisdiction Annual Conference, what frontiers remain for the church in race relations? As difficult as it seemed to be in 1964, it is easier to remove a racial structure than it is to overcome the social forces that caused the structure in the first place. Over the years of the debates on the Central Jurisdiction, James P. Brawley insisted that the basic issue was segregation.

Depending upon one's point of view, The United Methodist Church has come a long way since 1973. The Central Jurisdiction elected fourteen African American bishops during the twenty-seven years of its existence. The United Methodist Church has elected thirteen African American bishops since 1967. Before the church now are the tasks of living and acting as an inclusive church at all levels of structure and service. That has always been the task of the church. The demands of the twenty-first century will make this task an increasingly urgent one.

The story of the Central Jurisdiction as a structure began in 1939 with the adoption of the Methodist Plan of Union. However, the attitudes and social practices that prompted its creation go back into history, at least as far as the slavery controversies of the eighteenth and nineteenth centuries. As these attitudes changed—often by the force of legislation within the wider society and the changed minds of many people—the dilemma of the Central Jurisdiction was resolved.

Opportunities before the church are always better than dilemmas. What was feared in 1939 does not need to be feared any longer. As far as racial structure is concerned, The United Methodist Church can more faithfully seek the goal of one Shepherd, one fold.

NOTES

1. Edwin Holt Hughes, *I Was Made a Minister: An Autobiography* (Nashville: Abingdon Cokesbury, 1943), p. 281.
2. Methodist Episcopal Church Annual Conference, *The Daily Christian Advocate*, May 5, 1936, p. 88.
3. James S. Thomas, "The Central Jurisdiction: Dilemma and Opportunity." *Motive* Magazine, March 1964, p. 17.
4. *Journal of the Eighth Session of the Central Jurisdiction*, 1967, p. 73.
5. Ibid.
6. Prince A. Taylor, Jr., *The Life of My Years* (Nashville: Abingdon Press, 1983), pp. 76-77.
7. Ralph A. Felton, *The Ministry of the Central Jurisdiction of the Methodist Church*, p. 11.
8. Ibid., p. 01.
9. Ibid., p. 16.
10. Grant S. Shockley, Earl D. C. Brewer, and Marie Townsend, *Black Pastors and Churches in United Methodism* (Atlanta: Center for Research in Social Change, Emory University, 1976), p. 53.
11. *Journal of the Sixth Session of the Central Jurisdictional Conference of the Methodist Church*, p. 118.
12. Ibid., p. 72.
13. Letter from J. H. Graham to James S. Thomas, July 3, 1962.
14. Quoted in Dwight W. Culver, *Negro Segregation in the Methodist Church* (New Haven: Yale University Press, 1953), p. 77.

D uring my graduate school days (1950–53) I did not give much attention to the segregated structures of the Central Jurisdiction. Like many others, I felt deeply that segregation was wrong, especially in the Church.

It took some time before the Central Jurisdiction could begin to function as a jurisdiction. All other jurisdictions also had to learn how to function as jurisdictions but they did not have the added burden of being spread out over the United States.

As we have seen, the Central Jurisdiction was heavily opposed by the African American members of the Uniting Conference in 1939. But once the structure was in place, the members of the nineteen annual conferences decided to use it as best they could, until such time as the racial jurisdiction could be abolished.

Looking back over the twenty-four-year period when the Central Jurisdiction existed as an unbroken unit of nineteen annual conferences, I see three periods of emphasis. The first period, 1940 to 1948, was a time when the Central Jurisdiction learned to function as a jurisdiction. The second period began with James P. Brawley's resolution for the Central Jurisdiction to appoint its first committee. During this period, 1948 to 1952, many critical articles were written, speeches made, and resolutions passed, all aimed at the elimination of the Central Jurisdiction.

The period from 1952 to 1956 was a continuation of the story begun in 1948. In its report to the 1952 Central

Jurisdiction Conference, the Commission was forthright in its findings and recommendations. It said:

> There are two confessions which the Methodist Church in all honesty must make. The first is that the Central Jurisdiction as now constituted and operated is plain segregation, and that it is a carefully planned scheme to protect the general pattern of segregation. The second confession is that the Central Jurisdiction as a segregated unit is inconsistent with and in opposition to the tenets of the Christian faith. (Commission Report, p. 34)

This was as forthright a statement as leaders of the Central Jurisdiction had ever made.

The third period began with the passage of Amendment IX by the General Conference of 1956. This was a time when the church took seriously the means by which the Central Jurisdiction could be eliminated.

During my first General Conference in 1956, I was sitting in the gallery of the auditorium when Amendment IX was debated and finally passed. I was amazed at the timidity of the amendment and its awkwardness. Over and over, I heard the term "voluntarism" as if the church had all the time it wanted to make up its mind.

As a group of us left the auditorium, we were asked by a reporter how we felt. I told him that I felt very sad that the General Conference took so long to take any step toward the elimination of the Central Jurisdiction. At that time, I felt, along with many others, that the five or six steps of Amendment IX that had to be taken by a local church before it could transfer into another jurisdiction were too many hurdles to face. There had to be a better way.

The General Conference of 1956 took another step in which there was some hope. It authorized the Commission to Study and Recommend Action Concerning the Jurisdictional System. I had little hope that the Jurisdictional System would be abolished, but did hope for a clearer word on the elimination of the Central Jurisdiction.

I was sitting in the gallery, along with other General Board staff persons, when the Commission to Study the Jurisdictional System made its report to the 1960 General Conference. When I heard that no recommendation would be made for any change in the Central Jurisdiction, I felt very much as the African American members of the General Conference felt in 1939 when the Central Jurisdiction became a part of the Plan of Union.

Like so many other African Americans, I had been deeply moved by the bus boycott in Montgomery, Alabama in 1955 and other Civil Rights actions toward repeal of segregation laws in the wider society. Then, in February 1960, before the General Conference met in May, college students began to sit in at segregated lunch counters all over the South. Was the church unaware of these happenings? Or did "voluntarism" really mean "delay"?

At that time I had no idea that I would be called upon to head a Committee that would actually draft a plan for the effective use of Amendment IX by annual conferences. But the Central Jurisdiction Conference of 1960 felt the urgency to do something definitive about the problem of its segregated structure, and the Committee of Five was appointed in November of 1960.

During the four years that we worked in the Committee of Five, we felt an excitement about our task. Amendment IX had many flaws but it was the only instrument we had at that time.

Very soon in our deliberations, we came to the feeling that local church transfers, from the Central to other jurisdictions, was a very inadequate use of Amendment IX. We therefore centered our attention on the transfer of entire annual conferences, on a carefully made and sequential calendar. We also committed ourselves to do the planning and consulting with other jurisdictions to make this possible.

When Bishop Prince A. Taylor, Jr. went to New Jersey and I to Iowa in 1964, I felt that we had to assure the church, by the quality of our leadership, that the remaining annual conferences of the Central Jurisdiction could be transferred on schedule. Both of us expressed gratitude that the Methodists of New Jersey and Iowa had made up their minds that they would do all in their power to make our pioneering efforts a success.

Now, looking back over twenty-seven years, I am very grateful for the experience of being assigned to an Area which I did not know. I shall always be grateful to the Methodists of Iowa and of East Ohio for experiences which I shall treasure for a lifetime.

Black Bishops Elected by the Methodist Episcopal, The Methodist, and The United Methodist Church

Methodist Episcopal Church
Missionary

Name	*Year Elected*
Francis Burns	1858
J. W. Roberts	1866
Isaac Scott	1904
A. P. Camphor	1916

Methodist Episcopal Church
for
Black Annual Conferences

Robert E. Jones	1920
Matthew W. Clair, Sr.	1920
Alexander P. Shaw	1936

Central Jurisdiction
for
Black Annual Conferences

W. A. C. Hughes	1940
Lorenzo H. King	1940
Willis J. King	1944
Robert N. Brooks	1944
Edward W. Kelly	1944
John W. E. Bowen	1948
Edgar A. Love	1952
Matthew W. Clair, Jr.	1952
Prince A. Taylor, Jr.	1956
Charles F. Golden	1960

Noah W. Moore, Jr.	1960
Marquis Lafayette Harris	1960
James S. Thomas	1964
L. Scott Allen	1967

Black Bishops Elected by The United Methodist Church for Service in Regional Jurisdictions

Roy C. Nichols	1968
Ernest T. Dixon, Jr.	1972
Edward G. Carroll	1972
Edsel A. Ammons	1976
W. Talbot Handy, Jr.	1980
Melvin G. Talbert	1980
F. Herbert Skeete	1980
Felton E. May	1984
Woodie W. White	1984
Leontine T. C. Kelley	1984
Forrest C. Stith	1984
Ernest W. Newman	1984
Joseph B. Bethea	1988

Ministerial and Total Membership in the Central Jurisdiction (1940–1964)

Year	Effective Ministerial Members	Local Preachers or Supply Pastors	Total Members of Churches
1940	1,103	2,207	359,860
1941	1,532	2,134	338,724
1942	1,473	2,100	331,704
1943	1,539	n.a.	320,600
1944	1,479	419	346,076
1945	1,451	540	328,371
1946	1,427	528	346,369
1947	1,345	607	335,843
1948	1,263	574	339,779
1949	1,262	581	343,724
1950	1,262	569	346,945
1951	1,244	586	344,990
1952	1,241	579	347,053
1953	1,238	517	343,746
1954	1,225	559	352,107
1955	1,268	555	359,786
1956	1,239	541	352,107
1957	1,200	507	361,388
1958	1,170	519	364,689
1959	1,156	510	366,889
1960	1,155	535	367,340
1961	1,123	535	368,485
1962	1,119	546	368,811
1963	1,149	568	373,327
1964	1,058	550	373,595

Source: *General Minutes of The Methodist Church*

Active and Inactive Members
of the Central Jurisdiction
(1940–1962)

Year	Active Membership	Inactive Membership
1940	308,577	51,283
1941	284,014	54,710
1942	280,723	50,981
1943	282,688	47,912
1944	282,654	64,422
1945	259,629	68,742
1946	258,175	69,320
1947	264,965	70,878
1948	262,767	77,012
1949	264,806	78,918
1950	269,298	77,647
1951	266,917	78,073
1952	273,358	73,695

Source: *General Minutes of The Methodist Church*

B I B L I O G R A P H Y

BOOKS

Bennett, Lerone, Jr. *Before the Mayflower.* Baltimore: Penguin Books, 1966.

Brawley, James P. *Two Centuries of Methodist Concern: Bondage, Freedom, and Education of Black People.* New York: Vanatage Press, 1974.

Clark, Kenneth B. *Dark Ghetto.* New York: Harper Torchbooks, 1965.

Curnock, Nehemiah. *The Journal of John Wesley,* abridged. New York: Capricorn Books, 1963.

The Doctrines and Disciplines of the Methodist Episcopal Church. New York: G. Lane and C. B. Tippett, 1844.

Farmer, James. *Lay Bare the Heart.* New York: New American Library, 1985.

Frazier, E. Franklin. *The Negro Church in America.* Reprint edition bound with Lincoln, C. Eric. *The Black Church Since Frazier.* New York: Schocken Books, 1974.

Graham, J. H. *Black United Methodists: Retrospect and Prospect.* New York: Vantage Press, 1979.

Harmon, Nolan B., Jr. *Discipline of the Methodist Church.* Nashville: The Methodist Publishing House, 1940.

Hughes, Edwin Holt. *I Was Made a Minister.* Nashville: Abingdon Cokesbury, 1943.

Mathews, Donald G. *Slavery and Methodism.* Princeton, N.J.: Princeton University Press, 1965.

McClain, William B. *Black People in the Methodist Church.* Cambridge, Mass.: Schenkman Publishing Company, 1984.

Moore, John M. *The Long Road to Methodist Union.* Nashville: Abingdon Press, 1943.

Niebuhr, H. Richard. *The Social Sources of Denominationalism.* New York: Meridian Books, 1957.

Outler, Albert C., ed. *John Wesley.* New York: Oxford University Press, 1964.

Richardson, Harry V. *Dark Salvation.* Garden City, N.Y.: Anchor Press, 1976.

Rudolph, L. C. *Francis Asbury*. Nashville: Abingdon Press, 1966.

Singleton, George A., ed. *The Life, Experience, and Gospel Labors of the Right Reverend Richard Allen*. New York: Abingdon Press, 1960.

Smith, Warren Thomas. *John Wesley and Slavery*. Nashville: Abingdon Press, 1986.

Taylor, Prince A., Jr. *The Life of My Years*. Nashville: Abingdon Press, 1983.

Wilmore, Gayraud, Jr. *Black Religion and Black Radicalism*. New York: Doubleday, 1972.

Woodson, Carter G. *The History of the Negro Church*, 2nd ed. Washington, D.C.: The Associated Publishers, 1945.

JOURNALS, REPORTS, AND ARTICLES

Cameron, Richard M. "The Abolitionist Struggle in the Methodist Episcopal Church." in *The History of American Methodism*, vol. II. ed. Emory Stevens Bucke. Nashville: Abingdon Press, 1964.

Commission on Interjurisdictional Relations. Report to the General Conference of the Methodist Church, Chicago, Illinois, November 8-12, 1966.

Commission to Study and Recommend Action Concerning the Jurisdictional System, January 6, 1960.

Committee to Study the Central Jurisdiction. "Bridges to Racial Equality." Report to the Central Jurisdictional Conference, Daytona Beach, Florida, June 16-21, 1964.

Daily Christian Advocate, The. The General Conferences of 1940, 1944, 1948, 1952, 1956, 1960, 1964.

General Minutes of The Methodist Church, 1940-1964.

Golden, Charles F. and Thomas, James S. *Central Jurisdiction Speaks*. Central Jurisdiction Study Committee Service Department, Washington, D.C., March, 1962.

Journals of the Central Jurisdiction Conferences, 1940, 1944, 1948, 1952, 1956, 1960, 1964, 1967.

Journals of the General Conference of the Methodist Episcopal Church, 1840, 1844.

Journals of the West Texas Annual Conference, Ninety-fourth Annual Session, May 27-30, 1968; Ninety-sixth Annual Session, 1970.

Official Journal of the Lexington Annual Conference, Ninety-fifth Session, June 10-14, 1964.

Shockley, Grant S., Brewer, Earl D. C., and Townsend, Maric. "Black Pastors and Churches in United Methodism." Center for Research in Social Change, Emory University, Atlanta, Georgia, 1976.

Spellman, Norman W. Article on the General Conference of 1844.

Thomas, James S. "The Central Jurisdiction: Dilemma and Opportunity." Drew Gateway, Spring 1964.

I N D E X

Abolition, 21
Abolitionist, 18-19, 33
African American Methodists, 31
African American Mission Conferences, 45
African Americans, 25 26, 30-31, 40-41
African Methodist Episcopal Church, 30-31, 41, 60
African Methodist Episcopal Zion Church, 31, 41
Allen, L. Scott, 145-46
Allen, Richard, 27-31
American Colonization Society, The, 34
Andrew, James O., 24, 37-39
Annual Conferences, 50
Anti-Slavery Convention, 19
Anti-Slavery Society, 17-18
Asbury, Francis, 16-17, 30
Atlantic Coast Area, 108
Baltimore Conference, 17, 36, 38
Bell, C. Cooper, 88
Bennett College, 158
Bethune Cookman College, 158
Bible, the, 24
Bosley, Harold, 85
Bowen, J. W. E., 78
Brawley, James P., 43, 75, 81, 92-93, 106, 116, 130, 141-43, 157, 161, 163, 168, 170
British Wesleyans, 20
Brooks, Robert N., 70
Cameron, Richard, 18
Capers, William, 24-25, 35, 39
Carrington, Charles, 43

Cartwright, Peter, 35
Central Christian Advocate, 70
Central Jurisdiction, 26, 31-32, 42, 46, 49-60, 62-63, 65-78, 82, 84-87, 89-91, 93-96, 99-110, 115-18, 120-22, 124-32, 135, 138-39, 141-46, 148-52, 154-60, 163, 166-71
Central Jurisdiction Study Committee, 118-22
Central Jurisdictional Conference, 54, 58, 65, 67-69, 72, 77, 80-81, 106-7, 111-12, 121, 123, 128, 137, 143, 158, 161
Christian Advocate and Journal, The, 19, 22
Christmas Conference, 48-49
Cincinnati Exploratory Meeting, 120
Clair, Matthew W., 80
Clark College, 156-58, 163
Coke, Thomas, 16-17
Coker, Daniel, 30
Collins, John A., 37-38
Colored Methodist Episcopal Church, 60
Commission on Interjurisdictional Relations, 116-19, 122
Commission on Union, 40-41, 59
Commission to Study the Jurisdiction, 80-81, 92-93, 95, 107-12, 122
Committee of Five, 120-21, 125, 144, 151, 161, 164, 166, 172
Committee on Conferences, 86-87, 91